DO YOU KNOW....

- One person in every three will experience a panic attack this year.

- Dehydration, pneumonia, heart disease, and asthma are among the many physical conditions that can cause panic disorder symptoms.

- Panic disorder runs in families.

- The onset of panic disorder is associated with major passages in life.

- Some forms of exercise can trigger a panic attack . . . but one form can dramatically help you control panic disorder.

- Two new medications offer relief from panic disorder . . . and are even more effective when combined with supportive therapy.

FIND OUT MORE IN . . .

IF YOU THINK YOU HAVE
PANIC DISORDER

Look for these other Dell Guides for Mental Health

If You Think You Have an Eating Disorder

If You Think You Have a Sleep Disorder

If You Think You Have Seasonal Affective Disorder

If You Think You Have Depression

A DELL MENTAL HEALTH GUIDE

If You Think You Have

PANIC DISORDER

Roger Granet, M.D.,
and
Robert Aquinas McNally

A DELL BOOK

Published by
Dell Publishing
a division of
Bantam Doubleday Dell Publishing Group, Inc.
1540 Broadway
New York, New York 10036

ISBN: 0-440-22540-X

Printed in the United States of America

Published simultaneously in Canada

April 1998

10 9 8 7 6 5 4 3 2 1

OPM

This book is dedicated to:

The Granet women:
Valerie, Courtney, and Jamie
Lois, Vicki, and Gail.
Thank you for your boundless love.
And my patients—with respect.

Gayle Eleanor:
For your eyes, your poems, your love.

Acknowledgments

Special thanks are due to Robin Levinson for help on the psychotherapy chapter; to Judith Riven, for launching this project and keeping it afloat; to Clifford Taylor, M.D.; and to Laurie Martin and Lesley Meisoll, for sharp-eyed editorial support.

This book is written for educational purposes only and should not be used as a substitute for professional medical care or treatment. All readers should seek the guidance of a psychiatrist or other qualified health practitioner before implementing any of the approaches suggested in this book. All treatment information is based on research findings current at the time the book was written. All names of panic disorder patients and their family members have been changed, and some details were altered to further protect people's identities.

Contents

Foreword

Panic disorder is the severest form of anxiety. Of itself, anxiety is an experience everyone knows. It is as natural and predictable a part of life as joy and sadness, anger and happiness, passion and pain. Anxiety can be identified as apprehension, tension, uneasiness, disquiet, agitation, angst, or nervousness. Unlike fear, which focuses on a specific danger, anxiety often arises against an uncertain, perhaps even unknown threat.

Mental health professionals divide anxiety into *psychic* and *somatic* components. Psychic (or central) anxiety is an intense emotional discomfort experienced as dread, fright, or impending doom. Somatic (or peripheral) anxiety includes sweating, trembling, palpitations, chest pain, difficulty in breathing, and flushing.

Experienced by almost one person out of three each year, a panic attack is a discrete episode of extremely intense anxiety that comes out of the blue. It starts abruptly and builds quickly, peaking within a few seconds or minutes and abating within about ten minutes. In addition to the usual signs of heightened anxiety, a panic attack may induce a sense of losing control, "going crazy," or dying. A person who is subject to panic attacks with some frequency and who is persistently concerned about additional attacks or worries about their consequences is said to be suffering from panic disorder.

After several episodes of panic, an individual with the

disorder develops anticipatory anxiety—a profound fear that another attack may happen, for example, behind the wheel or at the movies. This anxiety can escalate into an intense, uncontrollable fear—technically, a phobia—that drives the person to avoid any and all places and events where an attack might occur, a behavior known as *agoraphobia*. The powerful interplay among panic disorder's three components—panic attack↔anticipatory anxiety↔avoidant behavior—creates the panic disorder triad.

Panic disorder is a devastating emotional disorder that can ruin lives, destroy careers, and shatter marriages and families. People with panic disorder are more likely to abuse drugs and alcohol, and they run an increased risk of suicide.

Panic disorder affects nearly six percent of the population. Women suffer from the disease two to three times more often than men, and it runs in families, although it also befalls people with no family history. Outside gender and family history, panic disorder knows no prejudice against race, socioeconomic class, or geography. It is an equal-opportunity mental health problem.

Despite the profound pain of this disease, there is good reason to feel hopeful about it. At least 90 percent of people with panic disorder can improve significantly through treatments based on solid research and expert clinical experience. This bad disorder has a good outcome.

Helping you find relief from panic disorder as soon as possible is the intent of this book. By learning about the disease, patients and their loved ones can achieve hope based on accurate information.

Although described by the medical community as far back as the Civil War, panic disorder has been well defined and closely studied only in the past twenty years. Once thought of as a form of generalized anxiety disorder, panic disorder was first listed as a separate illness in the American Psychiatric Association's 1980 edition of *Diagnostic and Statistical Manual of Mental Disorders*.

Panic disorder remains difficult to recognize as a distinct disease entity because it mimics many other medical and psychiatric disorders. Panic attacks can occur in any mental illness. And the physical symptoms of an attack may be taken as signs of a wide variety of medical problems, including respiratory disorders, cardiovascular disease, endocrine abnormalities and disorders, neurological diseases, withdrawal from alcohol or barbiturates, and intoxication with cocaine or other stimulants. Many people with panic disorder have undergone extensive, costly medical workups to search for the cause of their symptoms, only to come up with no answer at all. To further complicate this diagnostic puzzle, individuals often have both panic disorder and another medical condition.

Fortunately the medical profession has made great progress in diagnosing the disease. In addition, better education of primary care physicians and specialists, as well as public awareness about mental illness, have helped identify more and more people with panic disorder.

The possible causes of panic disorder may be divided into biological, psychological, cognitive, behavioral, and sociological. On balance, research data suggest that panic disorder has a complex and multicausal origin.

Biology clearly plays a role in the disease. Certain areas of the brain, in particular the locus ceruleus, appear to be involved. This area deep in the brain stem holds an enormous collection of cells that produce adrenaline-like chemicals such as epinephrine and norepinephrine, which are associated with the body's fight-or-flight mechanism—the flood of involuntary physiological changes in the body that rouse it against a threat. During panic, an "overfiring" of the locus ceruleus increases the production of epinephrine and norepinephrine, possibly leading to many of the physical symptoms of panic.

Additional biomedical studies have focused on GABA (gamma-aminobutyric acid), an inhibitory or "quieting" chemical messenger, or neurotransmitter. Research has also investigated serotonin, another neurotransmitter that appears to have far-reaching effects on mood, including anxiety and depression.

Psychological theories of panic stem from Sigmund Freud's original notions of anxiety. The father of modern psychiatry viewed anxiety as a signal from the unconscious that unacceptable conflictual desires, particularly those of a sexual or aggressive nature, were emerging into consciousness. Modern psychoanalytic theories continue to focus on unconscious conflicts, but they place more emphasis on loss and separation, as well as difficulties in interpersonal relationships, than Freud did.

Cognitive theories of panic reverse Freud's thinking. Where Freud argued that how we feel influences how we think, cognitive theory holds that how we think influences how we feel. The cognitive view of panic looks at distorted thinking patterns—in particular, how one views the body's physical reactions to the external world.

Behavioral views of panic disorder are similar to cognitive theories. Simply stated, an individual learns to be frightened and from that learning or conditioning comes to fear fear itself. Behaviorists also look for abnormal learned responses to relatively benign stimuli that exaggerate bodily reactions into dangerous and catastrophic events—essentially, making a mountain out of a molehill.

The last concept of panic causality is sociological. Epidemiological studies focusing on the environmental stressors that precipitate or exacerbate panic have found a relationship between panic attacks and stressful events like marital separation, starting college, a geographic move, or death of a loved one.

Mental health professionals have used this enormous body of research and clinical data to develop specific, focused treatments for panic disorder that yield improvement in up to 90 percent of patients seeking help.

Although traditional psychoanalytic treatment has not yet yielded impressive results, a new extrapolation of Freudian concepts is providing an exciting treatment option. Panic-focused psychodynamic psychotherapy (PFPP) uses traditional psychoanalytic concepts to explore unconscious conflicts about separation, independence, sex, and aggression in a time-limited manner. Although not yet systemically studied, this therapeutic modality shows great promise.

Biological treatment of panic employs a wide range of antidepressant and antianxiety medications. In the late 1960s, the tricyclic antidepressant imipramine (Tofranil) was shown to be highly effective in diminishing symptoms of panic. Imipramine and many other antidepressants, including various tricyclics and monoamine oxidase inhibitors (MAOIs), apparently work primarily on neurotransmitters (chemical messengers) that mute excessive activity in the brain. Recently, selective serotonin reuptake inhibitors (SSRIs), another class of antidepressants that includes the much-publicized Prozac, have also been shown to be effective in the treatment of panic. Additionally, a group of tranquilizers, or anxiolytics, such as alprazolam (Xanax) and clonazepam (Klonopin), which probably affect GABA, have shown excellent outcomes.

Cognitive-behavioral therapy melds the understandings of both cognitive and behavioral theories. The initial task of cognitive treatment is to identify distorted thinking patterns. Commonly the panic patient sees the world as overly dangerous and feels inadequate to deal with such danger. Another common distortion is viewing normal body functions as life-threatening—for example, perceiving rapid heartbeat after exercise as evidence of an imminent heart attack. The behavioral components of cognitive-behavioral therapy include relaxation training, breathing techniques, and a process called "flooding," in which the panic patient goes to a feared environment, such as the grocery store or a ballpark, and relearns that nothing terrible happens there.

Numerous studies have validated the effectiveness of cognitive-behavioral therapy and medication alone. Whether the two together constitute a more effective treatment than either separately remains to be determined.

The last therapeutic modality explores an individual's sociology, focusing on environmental stressors that may lie behind panic attacks. These stressors include real and symbolic losses and separations, such as emotional or geographic detachment from a loved one.

Panic disorder exacts an enormous emotional toll on both the patient and his or her loved ones. This book acknowledges and validates those feelings of fear, confusion, and helplessness. And by providing the most current data on diagnoses, causes, and treatments, it reassures those who suffer from panic disorder and encourages them to seek professional help.

Panic is a dark disorder. This book suggests a bright outcome.

Roger Granet, M.D., F.A.P.A.

Clinical Associate Professor of Psychiatry,
Cornell University Medical College
Morristown, New Jersey
August 1997

Chapter One

INTRODUCING PANIC DISORDER

> *"I'm just freaking, and I feel like my body's freaking out. I mean the shaking and the breathing and the sweats, and the heart and the pain in the chest—I feel like I'm going to have a heart attack or something. Except I never do."*

This is how one patient describes a panic attack, hallmark of the mental illness known as panic disorder. Frightening and deeply distressing, panic attacks are extreme expressions of anxiety. In panic disorder, panic attacks are repeated and seemingly random; they come out of the blue, for no apparent reason. The attacks are so disturbing that they lead to a profound fear of further attacks and come to dominate the way you live. Yet even though panic disorder is a serious disease, nine out of ten people with panic disorder who receive appropriate treatment can live normal, productive, and fear-free lives.

Is panic disorder a common disease?

Yes. The illness is more widespread than most people—including those who have it—realize. About thirty out of every one hundred people experience at least one serious panic attack in a given year. Full-blown panic disorder affects an estimated two to six percent of Americans, or approximately two to six people per hundred.

The reason for the difference in these two statistics is that a single panic attack does not necessarily signal panic disorder. The medical definition of panic disorder requires more than one attack. Usually psychiatrists look for a repeated pattern of unexpected episodes of panic. There is no magic number, but a pattern is required for a panic disorder diagnosis.

However, the "official" two-to-six-percent statistic for the incidence of panic disorder is certainly too low. Panic disorder can be difficult to diagnose because the symptoms imitate so many other diseases. One study found that people with panic disorder often see as many as ten physicians before their disease is finally diagnosed accurately. The same study also revealed that only one out of four people with the disorder actually receives needed treatment. People suffering from panic disorder are likely to be told they have something different, and the real cause of their suffering may go undetected. As a result of these findings, experts on panic disorder contend that the disease affects considerably more people than is generally thought to be the case.

As with all serious health issues, only an expert can determine whether panic disorder is present. Panic attacks can result from a number of mental health disorders, and they may arise from physical causes as well, such as thyroid imbalance or drug intoxication. There is no substitute for a thorough medical evaluation, preferably by a psychiatrist.

What does a panic attack feel like?

From a medical point of view, a panic attack is an extreme expression of anxiety. Everybody experiences anxiety from time to time—that uneasy, vigilant feeling that pushes us to take care of important business, on the job and at home. In your mind, anxiety makes you feel fearful, apprehensive, perhaps out of control. Your body expresses these feelings as clammy palms, dry mouth, butterflies in the stomach, and increased heart rate, among other signs.

In a panic attack, the psychological and physical symptoms of anxiety are vastly heightened—rapid heartbeat, shortness of breath, nausea, chills, and sweating, for example. Usually panic arises in a fearful situation, such as being confronted by a danger or threat. Imagine yourself going down in an airplane or facing a mugger pointing a cocked pistol at your chest, and you can feel the beginnings of panic stirring in your body and mind.

Panic is an expression of the body's fight-or-flight response—a set of profound involuntary physiological changes that occur whenever we face a stressful or threatening situation. A region of the brain known as the hypothalamus causes the sympathetic nervous system to release adrenaline (also called epinephrine), noradrenaline (also called norepinephrine), and related hormones that mobilize the body into a state of arousal and readiness. Metabolism, heart rate, blood pressure, breathing rate, and muscle tension all increase, preparing the body either to confront the threat or to run from it. Stories you may have heard or read about people lifting cars off trapped accident victims or outrunning a charging bull underscore the powerful, even life-saving effects of the fight-or-flight response in situations of danger.

In the kind of panic attack that characterizes panic disorder, however, there often is little or no external or objective danger—no airplane going down in flames, no mugger brandishing a pistol. The attack can happen anywhere, anytime, even during sleep, and the symptoms reach a frightening level. The attack comes on quickly, hitting a peak within seconds or at most minutes, and usually subsides fairly soon, although panic attacks can occur one after another over a period of hours or even days. People experiencing a panic attack often feel as if they are caught in a dream or an unreal state, and they may fear that they are about to die, go insane, or lose control.

A panic attack itself is not dangerous. But the experience is terrifying, largely because of the crazy or out-of-control feelings it arouses. And because people who experience panic attacks typically develop severe anticipatory anxiety about future attacks, their lives begin to change—very much for the worse.

What effect does anxiety about more panic attacks have?

Because panic attacks are extremely distressing, people with panic disorder can develop an overwhelming dread of the places or situations where they fear another attack might occur. Supermarkets, shopping malls, restaurants, churches, bridges, tunnels, classrooms and lecture halls, freeways, and airplanes are typical sites for panic attacks. They're all public places where personal space is unclear and escape routes are few. If someone suffers a panic attack in an airplane, for example, he or she may avoid future air travel out of fear of another attack. The same goes for freeway bridges over rivers or the checkout line at the supermarket. As the number of panic attacks mounts, so does the list of places to avoid. In extreme cases, the person is confined to home and is completely incapable of venturing outside. He or she becomes a prisoner of fear.

The three characteristics of panic disorder—panic attack, anticipatory anxiety, and avoidance—are linked like the three corners of a triangle:

PANIC ATTACK

AVOIDANCE   ANTICIPATORY
                             ANXIETY

This case history of a thirty-year-old college professor shows the complex interactions within the triangle of panic disorder:

Four months before the professor first saw a psychiatrist about his symptoms, he suddenly became "nervous" at a family picnic, and his heart began racing "a mile a minute." He broke into a profuse sweat, felt nauseous, experienced tightness in his chest, and had the sensation that he couldn't breathe, "as if someone was smothering me with a pillow." The attack came on for no apparent reason and lasted about fifteen minutes. The experience so terrified him that he asked his wife to drive home because he feared another attack behind the wheel. Later that same day, he experienced a second sudden bout of unexplainable panic while sitting on the porch with a neighbor.

Over the next few weeks he underwent a variety of

medical tests. The results were negative. Nothing was physically wrong with him.

But the professor kept having two or three panic attacks a week. He gave up driving because of his fear of having an attack in the car, and he started riding the train to work. Then he began experiencing attacks on the train. He took trains before and after rush hour because they were less crowded and it was easier to rush out of the car if an attack struck. Still his fear of panic attacks on the train finally grew so profound that he gave up riding the train as well and took a leave of absence from his job. Soon he could enter crowded public places like grocery stores and banks only if his wife went with him. He was essentially confined to his house, experiencing three or four panic attacks a week and living in constant fear that the next one would kill him.

The technical name for the professor's fear of crowded public spaces is *agoraphobia*. The word comes from the Greek, meaning "fear of the marketplace"—or any other large, public space outside one's own home.

Is agoraphobia always a part of panic disorder?

Panic disorder can occur with or without agoraphobia. But even without agoraphobia, the disease causes a high level of pain and suffering, and it badly disrupts the way people function in their daily lives.

This is a case history of panic disorder without agoraphobia:

A 26-year-old legal secretary experienced her first panic attack while watching television at home. The symptoms were classic: a rush of anxiety, pounding heart, gasping for air, chest pain, tingling in the fingers

*and toes, and violent shaking. The panic was over in
minutes, and she rushed to the emergency room immediately, fearing a heart attack. Tests were negative.*

*The second attack occurred five months later. She
was walking to her job, when panic overwhelmed her
out of the blue. The experience was so disturbing that
she took the day off to rest and recover.*

*It was only three months till the next attack, this
time in a supermarket. She dropped her groceries and
ran out of the store in a state of abject terror.*

*Now the attacks came more often, first weekly, then
daily, and finally several times a day. No matter where she
went or what she did, panic might strike at any moment.
She continued to go about the tasks of her life, but she
was so preoccupied with when and where the next attack
would happen that she was unable to focus on her work.*

In this case, the woman still commuted to her
job, bought groceries, went to the park and the post
office, and ate dinner at restaurants. She did not have
agoraphobia. Unlike the college professor, she could
leave home. But like him, she was preoccupied with the
attacks and was undergoing major distress and difficulty, both from the panic itself and from the inability
to concentrate on anything other than the time and
place of the next attack.

Does one panic attack mean I have panic disorder?

Not at all. To begin with, one panic attack does not
make a disorder. In fact, individual isolated panic attacks are relatively common, striking nearly one out of
every three people each year. The medical definition of
panic disorder requires more than one attack, and at
least some of the attacks must be unexpected. There is

no magic number, but a pattern is required for a panic disorder diagnosis.

And there's more to panic disorder than the panic attacks themselves. There also needs to be a period of fear about subsequent attacks or a significant change in lifestyle resulting from panic attacks. The case histories of the college professor and the legal secretary show how panic attacks become central in the lives of people with panic disorder.

Another important feature of panic disorder is the fact that at least some panic attacks are unrelated to fearful situations. They seem to come out of nowhere. That's what happened to the college professor at the family picnic and to the legal secretary watching television at home. The experience is so frighteningly powerful that a person with the disorder begins to reshape his or her life in an effort to avoid future attacks. This anticipatory anxiety and the avoidance behavior it leads to are as characteristic of the disease as the panic attacks themselves.

Can panic attacks be caused by something other than panic disorder?

Absolutely yes. A number of medical conditions can result in panic attacks. Examples are thyroid problems, certain brain and heart diseases, low blood sugar (hypoglycemia), and adrenal disease. Drugs can also cause panic attacks. Very large amounts of caffeine, marijuana, or cocaine, for instance, are toxic and can induce panic. Withdrawal from other substances, such as alcohol or narcotics, in addicted individuals may also trigger panic.

Panic attacks also arise from mental health problems other than panic disorder. Examples are depression, anxiety disorders, and phobias. What sets panic disorder apart is the unexpectedness of the attacks. Panic attacks in a phobia, for example, have an identifiable cause. Someone with a snake phobia can launch into a panic attack at the mere sight of a tiny garter snake in the grass. The snake itself offers no threat, but the attack has a clear-cut cause in the external environment. In panic disorder, at least some attacks happen without any apparent cause.

Because panic disorder can imitate other disorders and diseases, it is very important that anyone experiencing panic symptoms consult a medical professional. The best choice is a psychiatrist who has experience in diagnosing and treating panic disorder. In chapter 4 we'll discuss ways to find such professional expertise.

If the panic attacks in panic disorder come out of the blue and have nothing to do with fearful situations, aren't they just in the person's head?

Panic disorder is in the head, but it arises from complex interactions of the brain's chemistry and anatomy, personal psychology, and learned behavior. Panic disorder is a disease, not a failure of courage or willpower. It's as real as measles or mumps. You can't just wish the mumps away or tell the measles to beat it. The same goes for panic disorder.

Why worry about panic disorder? Does it pose a danger to the people who have it?

Panic attacks, and the fear they breed, are horrible experiences that no one should have to suffer. In addition, the consequences of the disorder are serious and can be life-threatening.

Very often panic disorder is not a stand-alone illness.

A number of physical and mental health problems develop along with or because of it. Physical symptoms can include chest pain, migraine headaches, irritable bowel, and asthma. In terms of mental health, panic disorder leads to major depression in 40 to 80 percent of all cases, creating an additional set of serious symptoms and issues. People with panic disorder often turn to alcohol or drugs in the hope of stopping the fear and anticipatory anxiety. They are at high risk for developing patterns of substance abuse that themselves are serious mental health issues.

People with panic disorder typically suffer from impaired health. One study found that people with the disorder went to the doctor or emergency room thirty-seven times a year—compared with five annual visits in the general population. Yet another study of 60,000 health professionals found that people who felt panicky in crowds, a symptom of agoraphobia, had a ten-times-greater risk of fatal heart attack than those who never felt panicky in a crowd.

Panic disorder also exacts tremendous social and personal costs. Often people with the disease cannot hold a job; fear locks them into their homes and leaves no energy for working. Careers may be ruined, and financial disaster can result, affecting not only the person with panic disorder but also his or her spouse and children. Major relationships, like marriages, often break down under the strain of the disease. Living with someone whose entire life is built around uncontrolled panic and the fear of that panic is demanding and difficult for spouses and partners.

Unsurprisingly, people with untreated panic disorder may decide life is too painful to continue. One large study revealed that individuals with panic disorder are twenty times more likely to attempt suicide than people with no diagnosed psychiatric disease.

Just who gets panic disorder?

Practically anybody can. The disease affects all races, social and economic classes, and geographical areas. Scientists have even discovered that the disease is equally commonplace in every country where it has been studied.

Usually panic disorder sets in between the middle teen years and the midthirties. It can arise both before and after this portion of the life span, but it is relatively rare.

Curiously, for reasons still unknown, panic disorder without agoraphobia is twice as common in women as in men. With agoraphobia, the disease is three times as common in women.

Panic disorder tends to run in families. If a member of your immediate family—parent, brother or sister, or child—suffers from panic disorder, your odds of developing the disease are four to eight times higher than someone whose family has no such history.

Do we know what causes panic disorder?

No single cause has yet been identified, and the disease probably arises from an interaction of factors. Basically, there are four points of view on the origins of panic disorder: psychoanalytic, cognitive, behavioral, and biological.

Psychoanalytic origin. According to a line of thinking that flows from the work of Sigmund Freud, panic is a signal that the ego is being overwhelmed by unacceptable or conflictual feelings, usually of a sexual or aggressive nature, that have long been repressed, or forced down out of consciousness. The ego perceives the emergence of these feelings into consciousness as a threat, and it responds just as it would to an external threat like a crashing airplane or menacing mugger. Panic serves as a sign that such a disturbing internal event is occurring.

An example would be a young man who has developed powerful feelings of rage against his spouse. Instead of expressing these feelings, he represses them, forcing them deep inside. When he is in his wife's presence, however, these feelings emerge, overwhelming his defenses and flooding into his consciousness. A panic attack begins.

Cognitive origin. Cognitive theory reverses Freud's thinking. Where Freud argued that how we feel determines how we think, cognitive theorists hold just the opposite—how we think determines how we feel. In cognitive theory, panic results from distorted, mistaken thoughts that lead to feelings of panic. A classic case would be someone who thinks that the labored breathing and slight wooziness resulting from running up four flights of stairs is the first symptom of an impending heart attack. Frightened by the erroneous thought that sudden death is only seconds away, the individual panics.

Behavioral origin. Behavioral theorists see panic disorder as the result of conditioning that associates two events. For example, a person may link the painful experience of a random panic attack with an unrelated event, like crossing a bridge. Thereafter, even approaching a bridge pushes the individual into extreme anxiety and may launch an attack. Avoiding bridges becomes a way of trying to avoid panic attacks.

Biological origin. The fact that panic disorder runs in families suggests an inherited physical mechanism that magnifies the ordinary signs of fear into frightening panic symptoms. Scientists studying the disease have found they can cause panic attacks in people who have the disorder by injecting certain chemical agents. The same chemicals don't have a panic-causing effect in people without panic disorder. And finally, the fact that panic disorder is equally common in every country where it's been studied points to a biological cause. If the cause were only personal, social, or cultural, panic disorder would be more common in some countries and less common in others.

It is possible that the biological root of panic disorder is the fight-or-flight response run amok. Some people may have an inherited susceptibility that makes their bodies overreact and pushes them into panic even when they are facing little or no threat. Scientists are currently investigating this avenue of research.

Do social or life events have anything to do with triggering panic disorder?

Psychological stress does play a role in bringing on panic disorder, possibly serving as a trigger to an underlying biological condition. A study in the 1980s by the National Institute of Mental Health revealed that 80 percent of people with panic disorder had experienced a powerfully stressful event soon before their first panic attack. In women, the event was usually related to family life, such as divorce or the birth of a child. In men, the event usually had to do with work, particularly a promotion or increased responsibility. With more women moving into the workforce over the past twenty years, there may currently be less gender difference in the kind of life events that can trigger panic disorder.

In both men and women, panic disorder often begins

in the early twenties, as people make the stressful transition from single or student life into the adult roles of marriage, family, and work.

How do other people react to someone with panic disorder?

Usually they have no idea what is going on. Because they don't understand the nature of panic disorder, they are likely to dismiss an attack as an irrational fear. They see it as an it's-all-in-your-head problem. "Can you believe it?" they'll say. "Fred won't use the subway because he's afraid of a panic attack," or "Lisa's stopped going to the supermarket because just the thought of leaving the house makes her break out in a cold sweat." Then they shake their heads in disbelief that somebody they know could be so silly, so frightened at just plain nothing.

People looking at panic disorder from the outside don't realize that the disorder doesn't result from a lack of courage or a failure of moral character. Because they fail to understand that panic disorder is a disease, they may turn on or abandon anyone who has it, further isolating that person and making his or her life situation all the more impossible.

This social isolation only makes panic disorder harder for the person who suffers from it. The disease itself makes it difficult to function in ordinary ways, like holding on to a job and playing a role in the family. When friends, family, and associates turn on a person exhibiting symptoms of the disease, he or she finds it an even bigger challenge to keep on living. This demoralization can be one of the events that triggers major depression and boosts the risk of suicide among people with panic disorder.

Can panic disorder be treated successfully?

Absolutely. In nine out of ten people with panic disorder, treatment will greatly improve quality of life. Panic disorder is recurrent in many cases—that is, it tends to come back—but the disease can be treated effectively and successfully whenever it appears.

Treatment consists of medication to alleviate the symptoms of panic attack, psychotherapy focused on recognizing the first signs of an impending panic attack and learning how to deal with them before they run wild, or a combination of both medication and psychotherapy. Given the right treatment by a medical professional who understands the problem, people with panic disorder can unlock their prison of fear and live much more normal and productive lives.

These case histories typify how panic disorder arises, how it is recognized, and how it can be treated.

A 21-year-old college senior was sitting in a restaurant after pulling an all-night study session when a wave of nausea, sweating, and tingling in his hands and feet swept over him. Certain that he was experiencing a heart attack, he rushed outside into the fresh air, where the symptoms soon subsided. He wanted to put the attack out of his mind, but he kept thinking about it, worrying that he had tasted death. The second episode happened three days later, as he was heading toward a lecture hall to take a final exam. Even though the attack passed within ten minutes, he was so upset that he was barely able to get through the test.

A medical examination at the university health service, including an electrocardiogram, revealed no abnormalities. A physician recognized that the student's discomfort was a mental health issue. He referred the young man to a psychiatrist.

Hearing about the two attacks in a short period of time followed by intense fear and anxiety over future incidents, the psychiatrist correctly diagnosed panic disorder. He initiated a two-pronged approach to treatment: medication and psychotherapy. The medication consisted of clonazepam, which controls anxiety, and Paxil, an antidepressant that is also effective against panic attacks. In the psychotherapy sessions, the psychiatrist, who had noticed how the student magnified small physical symptoms into major catastrophes, worked with him to make his thoughts more realistic. Within four to five weeks, the student felt much less fearful.

Panic first hit this 28-year-old anesthesiology resident as she was administering anesthesia during a complex surgical procedure. The attack began as extreme nausea and progressed into a horrific sense of being trapped in a dreamlike medieval chamber of horrors. Unable to leave the operating room because the patient's life literally depended on her, the resident somehow got through the incident.

Afterward she was deeply afraid that something terrible had happened to her and would happen again. As residents do, she consulted with other residents in various specialties to see if any of them knew what was wrong, but she came out normal on every test. Meanwhile, the attacks struck with greater frequency, first once a week, soon two and three times a week. She began drinking heavily as a way of warding off her feelings of anxiety and fear. It didn't work.

Finally, certain that she was going insane, she referred herself to a psychiatrist, who realized quickly that she was suffering from panic disorder. He prescribed imipramine, a proven antipanic medication. He also *explained—in the considerable medical detail one physician uses in talking to another—what was happening to her physically and how the medication would help.*

That was exactly what the resident needed. Because the medication gave her more control, and because the psychiatrist's medical explanation lent her an understanding of the disease process, she felt better almost immediately. Within three weeks she was dramatically more comfortable.

Only a short while after this 17-year-old high school senior got her driver's license, her parents left for a trip out of state. She was on her own for the first time in her life.

The initial panic attack came out of the blue, as she was watching TV alone. She hyperventilated, felt her blood pressure and heartbeat skyrocket, and had the eerie sensation that this was all happening to someone else. The attack scared her so badly that she refused to drive, certain that a similar episode behind the wheel would kill her. And she did experience more attacks, first at school, then at church. Preoccupied with the fear of future attacks, she stayed at home, refusing to go out unless her mother came along.

The family pediatrician recognized the problem as a mental health issue. He referred the young woman to a child and adolescent psychiatrist, who started her on a new form of treatment called panic-focused psychodynamic psychotherapy (PFPP). Drawing on Freud's insights about repressed feelings, this approach focuses on issues of autonomy and separation facing the individual. Over a period of months, without medication, the psychiatrist helped the young woman understand how the driver's license, her week alone, and her fast-approaching high school graduation had raised signifi-

cant, emotionally painful issues about separating from her parents to achieve personal independence. As the 17-year-old came to a deeper understanding of herself, the panic attacks became less frequent and finally disappeared, as did her agoraphobia.

How will this book help?

Principally it will provide solid, up-to-date information about a serious mental health problem that too often is misdiagnosed and misunderstood. With panic disorder, as with all mental health issues, knowledge is power.

Chapter 2 discusses the symptoms of panic disorder and provides a checklist to help distinguish panic disorder from other diseases that can cause panic attacks. Chapter 3 lists the causes of the disease in detail. Chapter 4 provides information on the diagnosis of panic disorder, detailing what will happen if you go to see a physician to determine whether you have the disease. Chapter 5 describes psychotherapy, which is part of the treatment for panic disorder. Chapter 6 tells about the different classes of medication also used in treatment. Chapter 7 discusses complementary, adjunct, and preventive approaches to treatment. Sources of further information, including books, Internet sites, organizations, and district branches of the American Psychiatric Association, are listed in the appendix.

Chapter Two

WHAT ARE THE SYMPTOMS OF PANIC DISORDER?

What is the principal sign of panic disorder?

The most obvious—and most disquieting—symptom of panic disorder is repeated panic attacks. Even one panic attack is an event too disturbing to ignore. The experience is so profound that anyone who experiences it won't forget it anytime soon.

What does a panic attack feel like?

A panic attack is a distinct period of intense fear, anxiety, or discomfort that comes on suddenly and hits its peak soon, usually within ten minutes. Typically the attack provokes an intense desire to flee one's surroundings.

Drawing from rigorous research based on valid and reliable scientific criteria, psychiatrists list thirteen symptoms of panic attack, of which at least four must be present for an event to qualify as a true panic attack. In addition to panic's intense fear, these symptoms are:

1. palpitations, pounding heart, or accelerated heart rate
2. sweating

3. trembling or shaking
4. sensations of short breath or smothering
5. feelings of choking
6. chest pain or discomfort
7. nausea or abdominal stress
8. feeling dizzy, unsteady, light-headed, or faint
9. feelings of unreality ("This seems like a dream") or depersonalization ("It felt like it was happening to someone else")
10. fear of losing control or going crazy
11. fear of dying (often from stroke or heart attack)
12. numbness or tingling, usually in the hands or feet
13. chills or hot flashes

The time span of the attack is important. Panic attacks come on suddenly and powerfully. They peak in intensity within seconds to a few minutes, then subside, usually inside ten to fifteen minutes.

Attacks of lesser severity, which exhibit three or fewer of the thirteen symptoms, do occur. Experiencing sweaty palms and waves of nausea all day long is uncomfortable, but it is not a panic attack. The symptoms are too few, and the timing doesn't fit the profile of panic attack's rapid onset and peak. Such episodes are called limited-symptom attacks, as distinct from true panic attacks.

Is a panic attack dangerous?

In the short run and of itself, no. Although a panic attack is highly distressing, it poses no increased danger of sudden death—even though people experiencing an attack often suffer from an intense fear that they are about to die. Still, a panic attack is a serious symptom that can signal major disease. And there may be danger over the long run that the sustained release of adrenaline caused by repeated panic attacks increases the risk of heart disease, high blood pressure, and stroke.

One thing is certain, however: Anyone who experiences a panic attack should consult with a medical professional.

Are panic attacks common occurrences?

Yes. The latest research indicates that, in any given year, almost one-third of the population experiences a panic attack. True panic disorder is much less common, affecting between two and six people per hundred, according to most estimates. Many experts think these estimates are too low, however, because panic disorder is often misdiagnosed.

Then one panic attack by itself is not a sign of panic disorder?

That's right. To qualify as panic disorder, the attacks must be recurrent. However, no one has determined exactly how many episodes it takes for panic attacks to be considered "repeated and recurrent." One thing is certain—a single panic attack by itself is not a sign of panic disorder.

Are the panic attacks of panic disorder more frequent or more severe than panic attacks arising from other causes?

No. Essentially, a panic attack is a panic attack, whether it arises from panic disorder or some other physical or mental cause.

Frequency and severity of attacks in panic disorder vary markedly. Some people report attacks once a week for months at a time; others tell of daily attacks over a period of weeks, separated by months with no attacks at all. In addition, people subject to panic attacks usually experience limited-symptom attacks as well.

Are there other symptoms of panic disorder besides panic attacks themselves?

Yes. How the victim of a panic attack reacts to the attack also plays a part in distinguishing panic disorder from other diseases involving extreme anxiety reactions.

In true panic disorder, at least one attack often prompts a month or more of intense worry and concern about subsequent attacks. This anxiety is typically accompanied by a strong fear that the next attack will be the one that causes death or pushes the victim into insanity—essentially a feeling of impending, inevitable doom.

Another common sign of the panic disorder is a drastic reshaping of lifestyle or behavior to avoid attacks in the future. In the case history of the college professor given in chapter 1, for example, he first quit driving, then stopped taking commuter trains, all because he feared more panic attacks. The effect on his life was such that he had to take a leave of absence from his teaching post—clearly, a drastic reshaping of lifestyle in an attempt to avoid the consequences of future attacks.

This interplay between panic attacks, fear of future panic attacks, and behavioral changes to avoid subsequent episodes of panic creates the panic disorder triad:

PANIC ATTACK

AVOIDANCE   ANTICIPATORY
                                      ANXIETY

The panic disorder triad typically reshapes personality over time, particularly when agoraphobia is part of the disease. Because of their dependence on others for help with the ordinary tasks of daily living, panic disorder victims often become dependent and clinging. And the constant worry about panic attacks breeds obsessiveness.

Can panic attacks have causes other than panic disorder?

Absolutely; panic attacks can arise from both physical and mental causes. To be sure that panic attacks are indeed the result of panic disorder, a physician must rule out these other causes. Sometimes determining the exact cause takes careful medical detective work.

Can panic attacks result from physical causes other than panic disorder?

A number of conditions, diseases, and syndromes have the potential of presenting with panic symptoms. They do not, however, cause panic disorder. Instead, they mimic many of the same symptoms or signs.

Impaired breathing. Asthma, emphysema, chronic obstructive pulmonary disease, and pneumonia, as well as other diseases that make breathing difficult or labored, may cause a smothering sensation that can prompt a panic reaction.

Heart disease. Numerous cardiovascular conditions mimic a panic attack. Symptoms of heart attack, for example, may include sweating, chest pain and discomfort, numbness or tingling (usually in the left arm), nausea or vomiting, and rapid heartbeat. Increased heartbeat (tachycardia) can cause palpitations. Abnormal heart rhythms (arrhythmias) or high blood pressure (hypertension) can also imitate the symptoms of panic disorder.

Endocrine abnormalities, changes, or disease. A panic attack often represents an extreme form of the fight-or-flight response that comes from the release of the hormones adrenaline (or epinephrine) and noradrenaline (or norepinephrine). Diseases that affect hormone-producing organs—the so-called endocrine glands—or changes in the normal functioning of these glands may lead to panic attacks. A thyroid gland that releases excess amounts of the hormones known as T_3 and T_4 can produce panic symptoms, as can an overactive parathyroid. A rare form of adrenal gland tumor known as a pheochromocytoma, which occurs most commonly in women between the ages of 20 and 40, may result in overproduction of epinephrine and norepinephrine and lead to symptoms that include anxiety with an impending fear of death, headaches, rapid heartbeat, sweating, flushes, trembling, and hypertension. Women going through menopause, with its many and often disturbing changes in endocrine function, sometimes experience panic symptoms, such as hot flashes, heart palpitations, and heavy sweating.

Metabolic disturbances. To work properly, the body must maintain a correct balance of certain salts, such as sodium, calcium, and potassium, known as electrolytes. Dehydration, among other causes, can disturb this balance and lead to panic symptoms.

Endocrine-insulin hormone imbalance. The hormone insulin, produced by the pancreas, keeps the sugar level of the blood within certain limits. If the blood sugar level drops too low, a condition technically called hypoglycemia can result, producing sweating, trembling, irregular heartbeat, and numbness in feet or hands. Hypoglycemia results from such medical conditions as insulin overdose, unusually heavy exercise in a diabetic person, liver disease (such as cirrhosis or hepatitis), and cancer of the pancreas. The opposite condition—hyperglycemia, which means too much sugar—may also cause paniclike symptoms. Hyperglycemia is most likely in diabetics, who produce little or no insulin.

Brain and nerve diseases. Multiple sclerosis, Alzheimer's, encephalitis, and similar serious diseases of the nervous system have the potential for causing panic symptoms. Seizure disorder, also known as epilepsy, focused in the region of the brain called the temporal lobe, can lead to panic attacks.

Vestibular dysfunction. The vestibular system includes portions of the inner ear and the brain that control equilibrium—keeping us upright when we walk and enabling us to tell up from down even in the dark or under water. Breakdown in the system can lead to vertigo (the room spins while you hold still), dizziness (the room holds still while you spin), vomiting, difficulty in coordinating movement, and anxiety.

Drug intoxication. A number of stimulant medications may cause panic reactions. They include over-the-counter decongestants, which can raise blood pressure and cause abnormal heartbeat; inhaled bronchodilators used to treat asthma; prescription steroids, which can mimic adrenaline and disturb normal endocrine functioning; and large doses of caffeine from coffee or stay-awake medications. Cocaine, which is a potent stimulant, can cause panic attack as well. Marijuana may also lead to panic, but the exact mechanism is unknown. Tetrahydrocannabinol (THC), the active ingredient in marijuana, is a hallucinogen rather than a stimulant.

Even certain herbal remedies sold as natural substitutes for synthetic medications may induce panic attacks. One is ginseng, usually from Korean sources. Another is ephedra, also known as ephedrine, ma huang, and epitonin. Both these substances have a stimulant effect that triggers the fight-or-flight response and brings on the symptoms of a panic attack.

Drug withdrawal. The sudden cessation of alcohol, sleeping pills and tranquilizers (Valium, Xanax, and similar medications), or opiates (painkillers such as morphine and heroin) may lead to panic symptoms, such as nausea, palpitations, heavy sweating, and fear of imminent death. This reaction is most likely in someone who is chemically dependent. Withdrawal symptoms sometimes appear in nondependent people who have been prescribed painkillers after surgery, even for a procedure as minor as root canal.

Are there psychiatric causes of panic attacks other than panic disorder?

Panic attacks can happen in any psychiatric disorder, more commonly in some than others. One of the most common is depression. Although we usually think of depression as a down or low-energy state, it can lead to agitation, such as sleeplessness, rising heartbeat, and heavy sweating. In some individuals, these symptoms may crescendo into a panic attack.

Panic disorder is usually classified as one of the anxiety disorders, and panic can be a symptom of these related diseases. Panic attacks also occur in people suffering from social phobias (abnormal fears of group settings like churches, sports arenas, and public speaking), specific phobias (abnormal fears of particular objects or situations, like snakes or elevators), obsessive-compulsive disorder (an extreme fear of, for example, contamination or infection through contact with other people), sleep disorders (such as *pavor nocturnus*, or night terror, in which the individual wakes up suddenly in fear), and post-traumatic stress disorder (powerful fear reactions caused by remembering a frightening event, such as a battle in warfare or being trapped in a wrecked automobile).

How do the panic attacks of these other psychiatric conditions differ from the panic attacks of panic disorder?

In terms of symptoms, they are no different at all. The college professor who had his first panic attack at a family picnic experienced the very same physical and emotional symptoms as the Vietnam War veteran who awakens in a panic from a dream memory of being trapped under falling napalm canisters. The racing heart, nausea, sweating, shaking, and fear of imminent death feel the same.

In the case of the Vietnam War veteran, the panic attack has a specific, clearly identifiable cue: the dream memory of a frighteningly horrific, near-fatal event. Similarly, a panic attack in an individual with a specific phobia about snakes has an obvious cue: say, a garter snake sliding through the grass.

In panic disorder, however, there's no "reason" for the attack. Feelings of panic descend unexpectedly, without a specific cue or cause.

So one of the symptoms of panic disorder is attacks that happen out of the blue?

That's right. Panic attacks in social phobia or post-traumatic stress disorder have a specific identifiable cue or trigger. By and large, an individual who suffers panic attacks from these disorders has some idea when they are most likely to happen. A person with a social phobia about baseball parks knows that going to Yankee Stadium has a high potential for triggering an attack. And a Vietnam vet who watches one of Oliver Stone's Asian combat epics realizes the film could elicit memories of battlefield horrors that bring on panic.

Mental health professionals distinguish three kinds of panic attacks. *Situationally bound (cued) panic attacks* occur almost invariably when the person is exposed to—or even anticipates—the cue or trigger: a snake in the grass, a baseball park, a battlefield scene. *Situationally predisposed panic attacks* are more likely to occur in a given situation, but not always and not necessarily immediately. A person who sometimes has panic attacks while driving and sometimes doesn't experiences this kind of attack. *Unexpected (uncued) panic attacks* characterize panic disorder. They come out of the blue, randomly, without a trigger.

However, distinguishing uncued attacks from the others is more difficult than it sounds. We humans are so good at coming up with explanations for events in our lives that panic disorder victims may decide that certain events trigger their panic attacks even when they don't. For example, an individual whose first sign of an attack is sweaty palms may say, "I get attacks only when my palms are sweaty," confusing a symptom with a trigger.

If you are suffering from panic attacks, the best course of action is to talk with a psychiatrist. He or she is trained to accurately diagnose types of attacks.

Does panic disorder affect men and women equally?

For reasons that remain unclear, panic disorder affects two to three times more women than men. Research points to possible biological and psychosocial causes for this gender difference. The greater amounts of the female hormones estrogen and progesterone in women may have something to do with the biochemical mechanisms that underlie panic attacks. Equally important, the social pressures placed on women, particularly their relative powerlessness and lack of control over their own lives, may lay the psychological foundation for panic disorder.

Does panic disorder run in families?

If you have a first-degree relative—a parent or sibling—with panic disorder, your chances of having the disease increase from four- to eightfold. However, panic disorder also appears in people from families with no history of the disease.

Is panic disorder more likely to begin at certain points in the life cycle?

Most people with panic disorder experienced their first attack between late adolescence and the midthirties. Onset during childhood or after age 45 is unusual but does happen.

Is someone with panic disorder likely to have other mental health issues too?

Panic disorder rarely occurs in isolation, all by itself. Many people who have the disease need to deal with other psychiatric problems as part of their overall treatment.

Drug and alcohol abuse is common among people with panic disorder, affecting 16 percent of people with the disease, according to one study. Alcohol is a common drug of abuse among people with panic disorder, as are tranquilizers (for example, Valium and Xanax). Opiates (heroin and morphine) and marijuana are also popular.

It isn't that people with panic disorder are junkies. Rather, some individuals try alcohol and drugs as ways of reducing panic's terrible discomfort. Many patients with the disease drop alcohol or drugs after a few experiments, but those who are predisposed toward addiction soon become dependent. In such cases, alcohol and drug dependence amounts to a separate disease from panic disorder requiring treatment on its own. Therapy for panic disorder won't make the drug addiction go away by itself. Typically Alcoholics Anonymous or some other twelve-step intervention is needed to break the chemical dependence and initiate recovery.

In addition, panic disorder is often accompanied by other psychiatric diagnoses. The most common is major depression. Related to common feelings of being down in the dumps or having the blues, major depression is a vastly more serious illness. From 40 to 80 percent of the people with panic disorder meet the criteria for major depression at some point in their lives. In about one-third of these cases, the depression came first and panic disorder followed. The remaining two-thirds develop depression after the onset of panic disorder, at least in part because of the demoralization and severe incapacitation that result from the disease.

Other psychiatric diseases may also appear in conjunction with panic disorder. They include obsessive-compulsive disorder, social phobia, specific phobia, and generalized anxiety disorder.

How can I tell if I am suffering from depression as well as panic?

Physicians checking for depression use a simple method of diagnosis. It's called SIGECAPS, a mnemonic that tells the symptoms to look for.

S   Sleep—insomnia or too much sleep
I   Interest—no interest or pleasure in life
G   Guilt—feelings of helplessness or hopelessness
E   Energy—no energy, listlessness
C   Concentration—difficulty in focusing
A   Appetite—increased or decreased
P   Physical activity—Either highly agitated and excited or withdrawn, rigid, and lifeless
S   Suicide—urge to destroy oneself

If five of the eight symptoms occur every day for two weeks in a patient who has been sad or blue for the same two weeks, and one of the symptoms is loss of interest, then the patient suffers from major depression.

Are suicidal feelings or suicide attempts an aspect of panic disorder?

Unfortunately, yes. The risk of suicide increases as a consequence of panic disorder. A 1990 study of 18,000 Americans in five cities found that the rate of attempted suicide among people with panic disorder was 20 percent—that's one in five—as compared with only a 1 percent rate, or one out of a hundred, among individuals with no diagnosed psychiatric disorder. Even when the researchers excluded the effects of drug dependence, depression, and alcoholism, panic disorder greatly increased the risk of suicide attempt.

Panic attacks are frightening events, and in panic disorder they descend without warning or explanation. Suicide is a radical, and final, way out of this seemingly inescapable, unexplained pain.

Suicide is one more good reason why anyone who suspects he or she has panic disorder should seek treatment. Therapy may save a life.

I have heard that people with panic disorder develop powerful fears about situations where attacks have occurred, sometimes to such an extent that they refuse to leave home. Is this true?

It is. So-called phobic avoidance—an extreme anticipatory fear of an object or situation—develops in 70 to 90 percent of people with panic disorder. Phobic avoidance develops from the panic disorder triad we've already discussed.

One of the symptoms of panic disorder is extreme fear about the next attack. A person who has suffered a panic attack in an elevator may stop taking elevators altogether. In fact, the very thought of stepping through the sliding door onto an elevator car can bring on extreme fear. This kind of abnormal, persistent fear is called a phobia. A person who avoids situations or objects that occasion a phobia is practicing phobic avoidance.

Agoraphobia is an even more heightened form of phobia's already-extreme fear, and it appears in 30 to 40 percent of panic disorder cases. Agoraphobia entails anxiety and fear about being in places that offer little or no chance of escape—except perhaps at the social cost of considerable embarrassment (for example, running out of a church, synagogue, or mosque in the middle of a worship service)—or where help is unlikely to be available in the event of a panic attack. Instead of the specific and limited situations that are the object of phobias, agoraphobia typically involves characteristic clusters of settings that entail being away from home alone, becoming part of a crowd, standing in line, passing over a bridge, and traveling in a bus, train, automobile, airplane, or other vehicle. To qualify as agoraphobia, the fear must be strong enough that the behavior is avoided altogether—by, for example, refusing to ever get on an airplane, train, or bus—or it is endured with serious distress and marked fear about a panic attack. People with agoraphobia often need the help of a companion to do even simple tasks like shopping for groceries or taking the subway to a doctor's appointment.

Is agoraphobia always a sign of panic disorder?

No. Agoraphobia can develop on its own, not as a result of panic disorder. Unlike people with panic disorder, individuals with agoraphobia alone don't experience true panic attacks. Their symptoms are more limited and less severe. In agoraphobia without panic disorder, the individual's fears focus on embarrassing paniclike symptoms—such as losing bladder or bowel control, vomiting, or feeling out of control—rather than on a full-blown panic attack.

This case history, of a 60-year-old woman suffering from agoraphobia alone, illustrates the difference:

At the age of 58, the patient—a widow who had successfully run her own growing business for fifteen years—began experiencing spells of dizziness that came on suddenly and lasted ten to fifteen minutes. Medical tests of her brain and vestibular system revealed no abnormality.

When the patient finally came to a psychiatric clinic, she had not experienced an attack of dizziness in over a year, but she lived in constant fear of further episodes. Desperately afraid that she would fall and end up disabled, she went nowhere without someone poised to catch her in the event of a dizzy spell. Although this woman remained an astute businessperson and continued a normal social life, her fear of dizziness pervaded her life and detracted from its quality.

Notice that this patient never experienced a full-blown panic attack. Instead, she had been through a number of uncomfortable limited-symptom events, which had prompted her fear of falling when alone. Additionally, her fear focused on the specific symptom of dizziness rather than on panic itself. She clearly suffered from agoraphobia, but without panic disorder.

What will happen to panic disorder symptoms if I simply wait and do nothing?

Sometimes panic attacks disappear spontaneously. However, untreated panic disorder is often a chronic disease that persists, in one form or another, for many years, even throughout one's life span. Panic attacks may rise and fall in frequency and severity over time, but usually they're not like a cold that clears up all by itself if you just wait long enough.

Remember too that untreated panic disorder carries with it a serious risk of other psychiatric diseases, such as depression, alcoholism or chemical dependence, and suicide. Ignoring panic isn't worth it.

How do I know if I—or someone I love—needs help?

Anyone who has a pattern of panic attacks, particularly attacks leading to major changes in lifestyle or to phobic avoidance, should seek professional help to determine their cause. Panic disorder is only one of the possible causes of such episodes. They may also result from a number of diseases and conditions, and they can signal mental health disorders other than panic disorder. If you, a family member, or a friend is suffering from repeated attacks of panic, it's time to talk with a mental health professional who is expert in anxiety issues and can diagnose the problem. Chapter 4 includes information on how to find and make use of such expertise.

Chapter Three

WHAT CAUSES PANIC DISORDER?

Why is it important to know what causes panic disorder?

It has been less than a quarter of a century since panic disorder was first recognized as a separate psychiatric disease, yet considerable research has since gone on in universities, medical laboratories, and clinical settings to uncover its causes and origins. There are three important reasons why this work is important—and even lifesaving.

First, determining the cause of the disease tells us more about how all of us—both those with panic disorder and those without—function as human beings. Scientific research provides important information about who we are.

Second comes the clinical reason. The better we understand panic disorder's causation, the better it can be treated. For example, if we understand the biological mechanisms underlying the disorder, physicians can choose the right medications to affect those mechanisms. Likewise, improved understanding of the mind's reaction to major life crises leads to more effective psychotherapeutic techniques.

Third and most important, understanding the cause of the disease can play an important part in recovery.

Our culture is unforgiving about what it perceives as emotional "weakness," treating panic disorder with reactions ranging from contempt to hostility. It is very easy for a person suffering from panic disorder to take on others' emotions and feel the same negative way about himself or herself. Small wonder that depression, drug and alcohol abuse, and suicide are all linked to panic disorder. A panic disorder patient who has an accurate, informed understanding of the cause of the disease stands a better chance of approaching life and treatment positively and effectively than does someone who has no idea where his or her panic disorder came from.

Does panic disorder have one clear definable cause?

Almost certainly not. Given what we now know, it appears that panic disorder springs from a variety of possible causes. Each of the theories that has been advanced to account for the disorder has at least partial validity, and some of the theories overlap in important ways. It's possible that they each explain the same cluster of phenomena from a different perspective and actually complement one another, adding to the richness of our understanding of how the mind and the body work together.

Basically there are five theories to explain panic disorder:

- biological
- psychological
- sociological
- cognitive
- behavioral

What does it mean to call a theory of panic disorder biological?

A biological cause is one that arises in the physical structure or chemical function of the body, particularly the brain. Essentially, biological theory considers panic disorder as an organic disease, much the same as multiple sclerosis, cancer, diabetes, or the common cold.

What is the biological theory of panic disorder?

There isn't just one biological explanation of panic disorder. Instead, scientists who have studied panic disorder from a biological point of view have developed two fundamental theories. The first concerns abnormality at the level of the nerve cells in the brain. The second focuses on the respiratory system and the acid-base balance of the blood.

Abnormality in the nerve cell complex. The basic unit of the entire nervous system is the neuron, or individual nerve cell. One neuron communicates with the next by releasing specialized chemicals called neurotransmitters. The neurotransmitters attach to specific areas on the nerve cell known as receptors and thus pass the information on. Put these three components together—neuron, neurotransmitter, and receptor—and you have the nerve cell complex.

A neurotransmitter can excite the next neuron in the nerve chain, or it can inhibit or slow that cell's action. The effect depends on which neurotransmitter is involved, which receptor it attaches to, and what chemical activity occurs inside the neuron. In terms of panic disorder, three neurotransmitters and one receptor are most important:

- norepinephrine—usually excites; triggers the fight side of the fight-or-flight response
- serotonin—excites or inhibits, depending on the receptor
- gamma-aminobutyric acid (GABA)—the primary inhibitory neurotransmitter
- GABA-benzodiazepine complex—a receptor closely associated with GABA; usually inhibits or "quiets" neuron activity

The first theory of the biological origin of panic disorder suggests that a nerve-cell-complex abnormality affects the fight-or-flight response in a way that produces panic. Say you're walking down a darkened alley, and a shadowy figure steps out from behind a Dumpster, flashing something that looks, even in the half-light, like a chrome-plated semiautomatic handgun. The locus ceruleus in the brain stem, which is rich in epinephrine- and norepinephrine-producing cells, releases these hormones, as does another region of the brain known as the hypothalamus. In response to the flood of hormones, the body mobilizes to arousal and readiness. Overall metabolism, heart rate, blood pressure, breathing rate, and muscle tension increase, preparing you either to face the threat of this would-be mugger or to turn and run away as fast as you can. Even after the emergency passes, you will for a while experience the heavy sweating, thumping heart, and rapid breathing that this aroused state induces.

Some researchers propose a different theory. They say that norepinephrine activity at the neurotransmitter-receptor level—called the *noradrenergic system*—is abnormal in certain areas of the brain. Because of this abnormality, any real or perceived threat sets off a profound overreaction, which leads to a panic attack.

Yet another idea is that the abnormality affects the activity of serotonin at the neurotransmitter-receptor level—called the *serotonergic system*. This abnormality prompts a similar overreaction, likewise leading to a panic attack.

Interesting laboratory evidence supports the theory of a neurotransmitter-receptor abnormality in the neurons of the panic-producing regions of the brain. Injecting panic disorder patients with certain drugs that act on neurotransmitter-receptor systems induces panic attacks that patients say feel just the same as panic episodes outside the laboratory. Yohimbine (Yocon), which stimulates the release of norepinephrine, can trigger panic attacks, underscoring the role of that neurotransmitter in producing panic symptoms. Flumazenil (Mazicon), which affects the production of the neurotransmitter GABA and affects the benzodiazepine receptor, also induces panic. This indicates that dysfunction of the GABA-benzodiazepine system plays into panic attacks.

Further evidence comes from the medications used to treat panic disorder. Drugs that affect certain neurotransmitters and receptors have been shown to be highly effective against the disease. For example, imipramine (Tofranil), the first compound used against panic, is an antidepressant that works by affecting the level of norepinephrine in the nerve cell complex. Diazepam (Valium) and related compounds, which attach to the benzodiazepine receptors on brain nerve cells and increase the release of GABA, reduce anxiety and panic attacks. Clearly, the benzodiazepine receptor has something to do with the disease. Likewise, selective serotonin reuptake inhibitors (SSRIs), the group of antidepressant medications that includes the well-known Prozac, have also been shown to stop panic. Since these medications affect the neurotransmitter serotonin, it appears likely that the serotonergic system plays a role in panic disorder.

Possibly all these drugs remedy or cancel some abnormality that underlies the disease and thus stop panic attacks. The abnormality may be either qualitative—that is, there's something chemically wrong with the neurotransmitters or the receptors, causing them to interact in an unusual manner—or quantitative—that is, there's too much or too little of a particular neurotransmitter, for example. We will look at these compounds and their effects in more detail in chapter 6, which covers antipanic medications.

Abnormal respiration and acid-base balance. Breathing takes in oxygen and releases carbon dioxide (CO_2). Carbon dioxide dissolves in the blood in the form of carbonic acid, so that blood carrying a large concentration of CO_2 is mildly acidic. By contrast, blood rich in oxygen is slightly alkaline, or basic. A respiration center in the region of the brain called the medulla oblongata monitors the acid-base balance of the blood and increases or slows the breathing rate to maintain a correct oxygen-CO_2 ratio.

The second theory of the origin of panic disorder puts the cause of the disease in the acid-base system governing respiration. According to this model, when the blood moves into the acid zone, it sets off a false suffocation alarm. Reacting as if the body were smothering when in fact nothing is wrong, the medulla oblongata tells the lungs to work at high speed. The individual feels short of breath, has difficulty breathing, and hyperventilates involuntarily, which leads to faintness, dizziness, a sensation of suffocation, and tingling in the hands and feet. These feelings combine with the rapid breathing and quickly escalate into a full-blown panic attack.

Laboratory researchers testing this theory have found that they can induce panic attack by injecting patients with compounds that upset the acid-base balance of the blood. Sodium lactate, an acid produced by the body, and sodium bicarbonate, another body by-product, have both produced this effect, as has carbon dioxide.

One of the most fascinating findings of this research is that sodium lactate injection sets off a panic attack in 80 percent of people with panic disorder but in only 20 percent of individuals without the disease. Apparently panic symptoms easily escalate into a full-blown attack in people with panic disorder, less easily in those without the disease. The reason this happens, however, remains unknown.

Other research reveals that some people with panic disorder show decreased levels of carbon dioxide and bicarbonate in the blood, a sign of physiological reaction to higher-than-normal levels of these compounds. This finding fits with laboratory research into panic, and it supports the idea that disruption of the body's normal acid-base balance plays some role in panic disorder.

Is there any additional evidence to support a biological theory of the disease?

Data from a number of other sources point toward a biological cause of panic disorder.

Family and twin studies. Various studies have found that first-degree relatives (brothers, sisters, children, and parents) of panic disorder patients have a four- to eightfold higher risk of suffering from the disease themselves. This finding could indicate an inherited propensity to panic disorder, a conclusion supported by limited research among twins. If one identical twin has panic disorder, the other twin, who is genetically identical, has a 30 percent risk of also having the disease. That's higher than the 10 to 20 percent rate for first-degree relatives, who are not genetically identical. Clearly, panic disorder or a tendency to the disease is partially inheritable. Inheritability points toward—but does not prove—a biological component of the disease.

Behavioral inhibition. Different people react differently to new people and objects. Some are drawn toward anyone or anything novel, while others withdraw, stop what they were doing, and seek comfort from a person they know—a personality pattern called behavioral inhibition. There is evidence that behavioral inhibition in humans is inherited; research shows that identical twins are more likely to share the trait than nonidentical twins. Behavioral inhibition may increase susceptibility to anxiety disorders, including panic. One study discovered that 85 percent of the children of parents with panic disorder displayed behavioral inhibition, as compared to 15 percent of the children of parents who did not suffer from any psychiatric disease.

Again, the inheritability of behavioral inhibition points toward a biological element in panic disorder. Perhaps, for example, a genetically based abnormality of the serotonergic or noradrenergic system underlies behavioral inhibition and contributes to the development of panic disorder.

Physical findings. Some studies reveal that people with a condition known as mitral valve prolapse may have a higher-than-normal incidence of panic disorder. The mitral valve separates the two chambers on the left side of the heart. In about five percent of the general population, this valve bulges down into the lower chamber, an abnormality called prolapse. Mitral valve prolapse is usually a benign disorder that causes little or no problem. Sometimes, though, it leads to infection of the heart muscle, strokes before the age of 45, cardiac arrhythmias, and short-term episodes of strokelike symptoms (called transient ischemic attacks) or blindness. Mitral valve prolapse also produces heart palpitations, which are a cardinal symptom of panic attack.

Evidence on the role of mitral valve prolapse in panic disorder, however, is contradictory. Owing most likely to the different research techniques used in different studies, the prevalence of mitral valve prolapse in panic disorder patients varies from zero to 50 percent—a wide range from none at all to one in every two. Clearly, this is an area that needs more research before the actual contribution of mitral valve prolapse to panic disorder can be defined.

Another area that needs more investigation is irritable bowel syndrome. Again, some studies indicate that people with this condition suffer more panic disorder than the general population. The mechanism for this effect, as with mitral valve prolapse, is unknown.

Brain studies. One of the most exciting technological breakthroughs during the past twenty years has been the development of methods for looking into the brain without opening the skull.

Two of these technologies, one called positron emission tomography (PET) and the other known as single-photon emission computed tomography (SPECT), actually allow scientists to observe how the brain functions. PET and SPECT studies have found that patients with a particular pattern of blood-flow into the brain's temporal lobe are more susceptible to laboratory-induced panic attacks than are people without the pattern.

Two other technologies—computed axial tomography (CAT) and magnetic resonance imaging (MRI)—allow detailed investigation of brain structure. Both CAT and MRI studies point to the existence of temporal lobe abnormalities in patients with panic disorder. These results remain preliminary, however, and further research is needed.

Researchers are also investigating the role of the locus ceruleus (Latin, meaning "blue place"), a pigmented structure located within the brain stem. The locus ceruleus is richly supplied with cells that produce norepinephrine, which prompts the fight-or-flight response. It is possible that some kind of malfunction in the locus ceruleus could precipitate panic attacks by flooding the body with norepinephrine. Research carried out in Sweden shows that the locus ceruleus reacts not only to external threats but also to internal alarms, such as the physical signs of smothering or difficult breathing. This finding lends additional support to the idea that a false suffocation alarm might trigger a panic attack.

Age of onset. One of the striking facts about panic disorder is that it begins only rarely in childhood and starts most commonly between the late teens and midthirties. First panic attacks after age 45 are rare, and the severity of attacks tends to diminish in the fifties and sixties. These data fit with known developmental changes in the human body. As we age, cognitive functions decline and the extreme excitement of neurons that can lead to panic declines. The age pattern shows how brain-centered and body-based panic disorder is.

What does it mean to call a theory of panic disorder psychological?

The biological theory looks for panic disorder's origins in the body's chemistry, physiology, and structure. The psychological theory places it in what we think of as the mind and the personality, sometimes called the psyche.

What is the psychological theory of panic disorder?

Psychological theories of panic and other anxiety disorders derive originally from the work of Sigmund Freud (1856–1939), the Austrian neurologist who developed the therapeutic method of classical psychoanalysis based on his extensive study of the mind's inner workings.

Early in his career, Freud considered panic attacks physical or biological events. But later on he adopted the view that panic, like much of human personality, results from what he called repression—the process by which the mind buries unacceptable feelings deep in the unconscious.

Individuals use repression, Freud said, to maintain their psychological balance, an activity that begins very early in childhood. When dangerous or unsettling feelings arise—like sexual urges toward a playmate, or a desire to kick and bite a parent—the child may unconsciously bury them as a way of eliminating the distress caused by the unacceptable emotions. Repression is one way the psyche ensures that difficult, conflictual feelings are put out of sight and kept out of mind.

Useful though repression may be as a coping mechanism, however, it can cause considerable anguish and suffering. Teeming beneath the surface, repressed feelings suck away psychic energy. And they may suddenly break into consciousness, threatening to overwhelm the mind's carefully constructed defenses against them.

Panic, Freud explained, is one way the mind reacts when repressed feelings invade the conscious mind. As far as the mind is concerned, repressed sexual or aggressive desires are every bit as threatening as a mugger brandishing a weapon or a tiger in ambush coiled to spring. Faced with a threat, the fight-or-flight response kicks in. In a person predisposed toward panic, an attack can occur.

How has the psychological theory changed since Freud's time?

Many psychoanalysts—psychiatrists and psychologists who follow Freud's method of therapy—still follow his basic construct of repression, but they have tended to move away from his focus on sex and aggression in early life. Instead, they look much more at feelings of loss and separation, both during childhood and in the patient's contemporary life, and on difficulties in relationships. They pay particular attention to separation anxiety, which refers to the level of distress an individual feels when out of contact with a significant relationship, such as parent or spouse. Separation anxiety overlaps somewhat with behavioral inhibition in that it also predisposes to shyness, clinging to a known authority figure, and fear of novel objects and people. In psychoanalytic terms, separation anxiety is often rooted in the child's deep fears of losing his or her parents, feelings that were and are repressed. Later events, particularly ones that mark major life changes—such as graduating from college, getting married, or having a child—can dredge these repressed feelings out of the unconscious, potentially prompting the onset of panic.

Does research support the psychological theory of panic disorder?

Some of the most interesting work from a psychological perspective has been done by Fredric Busch, M.D., Arnold Cooper, M.D., Barbara Milrod, M.D., and Theodore Shapiro, M.D. These researchers report that people with panic disorder share important traits—personality problems, troubled relationships, difficulties in handling certain kinds of emotional experiences, and conflicts about separation, anger, and conflict. Most of the patients studied had great difficulty expressing anger—often a sign of deep repression—and all had severe problems in their family or work lives. These traits predispose individuals to panic.

Busch and his scientific colleagues also found that all the patients they studied had endured a significantly stressful event within the few months before the onset of panic disorder. Typically this stress involved a change in the expectations put on the patient—for example, increased responsibility at work, or impending graduation from college. Patients linked such life changes to traumatic events in early life when parents frightened or rejected them as children and they became angry over this treatment. Afraid that the angry fantasies were actually capable of destroying the parent—a common belief among children—they unconsciously repressed their feelings as dangerous and fearful. Subsequent events that prompt anger resurrected this original fear and built anxiety to the level of panic.

In the view of Busch and his colleagues, people with panic disorder may be genetically predisposed to the disease, a tendency indicated by behavioral inhibition. Or it may be that trauma itself changes the way the fight-or-flight response works in the individual's brain and body and makes a panic reaction more likely.

Other research indicates that people with anxiety disorders, including panic, typically endured difficult childhoods. Onset of the disease in adolescence or adulthood may have its origins in events that happened years before.

What kinds of childhood events could establish a psychological tendency toward panic disorder?

As we have seen, panic disorder and related mental health problems tend to run in families. The biological explanation for this fact is that parents, children, and siblings share a genetic tendency to the disease. Psychological theorists point out that the experience of being raised in families with certain characteristics can seriously affect how a child reacts to feelings of stress.

Physical and sexual abuse. Although abuse history in panic patients has yet to be explored in depth, one study suggests that 60 percent of people with the disease have been the victims of abuse at an early age. Other studies indicate that abuse is common among people with anxiety disorders.

All abuse experiences entail an overwhelming feeling of powerlessness and loss of control. Potentially, adults who have been abused as children relive those frightening emotions when they again experience powerlessness or loss of control—for example, in a work situation. Or the original trauma may have made them exquisitely sensitive to stress and anxiety in a way that eventually leads to the onset of panic disorder.

A mentally ill and/or chemically dependent parent. Psychiatrically diseased mothers and fathers can teach children their own dysfunction. The parent models negative behaviors and expects the child to behave the same way, which he or she learns to do. The abuse of alcohol and/or drugs creates a family system that leads to uneven, unavailable parenting. Children have to fend for themselves emotionally while the mother or father is lost to intoxication. Separation, and the anxiety it spawns, is part and parcel of life in a family with a chemically dependent parent.

Parenting style. One study reports that patients with panic disorder, like those with major depression, described their parents as either cold and withdrawn or overly protective. Another research project found that what the researchers called affectionless control was the most common parenting style in the childhood families of anxiety disorder patients. Dysfunctional parenting is a common theme in the life histories of anxiety disorder patients, including those with panic, indicating the importance of these early-life experiences to psychiatric diseases that may not manifest themselves until years later.

Adults who were raised as children under such parenting styles often remember being extremely fearful of school or staying overnight with friends. These memories signal a high degree of separation anxiety, which plays into the development of panic disorder.

What does it mean to call a theory of panic disorder cognitive?

In the language of psychiatry and psychology, cognition refers to awareness through thought or perception. It

includes all aspects of thinking, perceiving, remembering, and thinking. In the widest sense, cognition covers
the processing of knowledge, the formation of beliefs,
and the development of thoughts about ourselves, the
environment, and the future. Cognition is largely conscious; we know when we are thinking, for example.

Originated by Aaron Beck, M.D., of the University
of Pennsylvania, cognitive theory developed in part as
a reaction to Freud's emphasis on the unconscious. It
basically reverses the formulation of psychoanalysis.
As Freud and psychoanalysis see the human mind,
emotions that are hidden away in the unconscious
and are attempting to break into consciousness control our lives. In short, how we feel determines how
we think.

Cognitive theory turns this around. It maintains that
our beliefs about ourselves and our world affect our
emotions. In short, how we think determines how we
feel. If our thinking helps us get along in the world,
then it is healthy and adaptive. But if it gets in the
way or causes distress, then cognition is unhealthy and
maladaptive.

What is the cognitive theory of panic disorder?

The key to a cognitive understanding of the disease is
understanding how the mind reacts to and interprets
events in the body. If, for example, you have been told
by a track coach that having a rapid heartbeat after
running four miles is normal, you're unlikely to think of
a faster, stronger pulse as anything more than tempo-
rarily uncomfortable. But if, for some mistaken reason,
you have the idea that an accelerated heartbeat is the
first sign of a fatal heart attack, you could become
frightened and anxious.

Cognitive theory holds that this kind of mistaken reading of physical events—which is called catastrophic misinterpretation—is the key to panic disorder. In a person with the disease, the misreading is enormously out of touch with any real danger, and panic results. Catastrophic misinterpretation is something like making a mountain out of a molehill because of a misunderstanding.

Working with maladaptive cognition, panic patients see the world as inherently dangerous, threatening, and frightening. They also perceive themselves as weak, and powerless, and unable to cope. Overcome by desperation and distrusting of their own ability to handle the situation, patients react emotionally with panic.

Why doesn't catastrophic misinterpretation happen to everyone?

Panic disorder affects some people rather than others, according to cognitive theory, because they are more highly sensitive to the signs of anxiety. Whereas most people might write off sweaty palms or butterflies in the stomach before speaking in public as simple stage fright, a person highly sensitive to anxiety would detect every small nuance of the sweating and the upset stomach, then magnify the discomfort into an impending heart attack or a stroke, heightening an ordinary fear into full-blown panic.

Is there evidence to support the cognitive theory?

Therapeutic approaches to panic disorder based on cognitive theory help patients identify the mistaken beliefs and bring their thinking back into line with reality. These techniques have demonstrated some success.

However, cognitive theory doesn't account for all

panic attacks. The key element of cognitive theory is the thinking mind. If the mind isn't thinking, obviously beliefs can't come into play and affect behavior. Therefore, if cognitive theory alone is accurate, panic attacks should not occur when the mind isn't thinking.

But they do. During sleep, the brain passes through nondreaming periods when its thinking regions are neither involved nor aware. Yet it is well documented that panic disorder victims have attacks during such dream-free, belief-free sleep.

Additionally, research into the life histories of many panic disorder patients fails to reveal any catastrophic misinterpretation of anxiety symptoms. Most panic disorder patients are as realistic in their descriptions of the body's reactions as are people without the disease.

What does it mean to call a causal theory of panic disorder behavioral?

Behavioral theory is closely related to cognitive theory. In fact, sometimes the two approaches are lumped together as cognitive-behavioral theory. Behavioral theory, however, puts less emphasis on beliefs, focusing on the ways we learn, often unconsciously, to associate events.

The most basic point of behavioral theory is that everything we do—whether healthy or unhealthy, adaptive or maladaptive—is learned. The physical and social environments shape learning. If, as a child, you screamed in a parent's face and were scolded in return, you learned that screaming in an adult's face can cause painful punishment in the form of disapproval. But if you kissed the adult and you were hugged back, then you learned that affectionate behavior is rewarded with the pleasure of more affection.

Freudian psychological theory emphasizes the unconscious emotional constructs within an individual. It wants to know how a person is put together before an action, such as a panic attack, occurs. Behavioral therapy looks instead at the consequence of the action. It emphasizes what happens afterward.

What is the behavioral theory of panic disorder?

Actually, there are three related ideas, each based on a particular type of learning.

Operant conditioning. Championed and popularized by the American psychologist B. F. Skinner, this theory holds that our lives are shaped by the rewards and punishments we receive from outside sources. The example of the child alternately screaming and hugging is a case of operant conditioning. The punishment negatively reinforces the scream in the face; as a result, further screaming is less likely. The hug positively reinforces the kiss; as a result, the child will probably want to kiss more.

Emotions arise in response to these reinforcements. The child feels positive and good about kissing the adult because hugging is the reward. But negative emotions, like guilt and fear, come from the punishment.

In terms of operant conditioning, panic disorder is seen as a learned pattern of behavior that continues because it is reinforced by the social or physical environment. Panic arises because it is a learned physical and psychological response to a particular stimulus—perhaps a bridge or tunnel, perhaps the thought of getting on an airplane, perhaps simply the feeling of being trapped and unable to escape. Something in the environment serves as a cue to which the person responds with panic.

Classical conditioning. In the early years of this century the Russian physiologist Ivan Petrovich Pavlov (1849–1936) demonstrated how the body and mind can learn to link two previously unassociated events and respond to the one as if it were the other. Working with dogs as experimental subjects, Pavlov rang a bell each time he presented the animals with their daily bowl of kibble. Seeing and smelling the food, the dogs salivated in anticipation as the bell was ringing. After doing this a few times, Pavlov simply rang the bell, without any food present, and the dogs salivated just as if the kibble were on its way to them. He had taught them to respond to the bell in the same way they would have behaved toward food. Such an association of events is called Pavlovian, or classical, conditioning.

Some behavioral scientists argue that classical conditioning underlies panic attack. The first step toward panic disorder begins when an individual associates an unpleasant or noxious event with a specific situation and fears the one because of the other—perhaps a wave of nausea while driving across a bridge, or an accidental electrical shock while reaching into a cold case at the grocery store. Thereafter the person reacts with fear to the prospect of going across a bridge or shopping for groceries. The second step to panic disorder occurs when the person begins to avoid bridges and grocery stores as a way of circumventing the fear response, and develops phobic avoidance.

The fear-of-fear principle. This idea takes classical conditioning a step further, recognizing the fact that panic disorder patients are more frightened of internal events, specifically panic attacks themselves, than of external situations. According to this model, the individual learns to associate a harmless internal physical sensation—say, mild dizziness—with an impending panic attack and takes the one as an invariable signal for the other based on learned fear. People with panic disorder constantly monitor their bodily responses and are so deeply fearful of panic attacks that their anxiety escalates out of control at the first sign that one is about to happen. It is like a circle that feeds on itself: fearing an attack prompts the attack.

Is there evidence to support the behavioral theory of panic disorder?

Like cognitive theory, yes and no. As we will see in chapter 5, behavioral therapy can be a successful way to treat panic disorder, a fact that indicates at least some accuracy in the theory.

In terms of research, an interesting study showing how classical conditioning contributes to the development of panic disorder was conducted at Princeton University by Barry Jacobs, Ph.D. He exposed cats to both a tone, which is neutral to the animals, and a puff of air, which they regard as a threat. The puff of air, Jacobs showed, activates the locus ceruleus, the portion of the brain that produces adrenalinelike hormones involved in the fight-or-flight response. After repeated pairings of the tone and the puff of air, the tone alone activated the locus ceruleus. This finding shows that the portion of the brain critical to panic disorder can be classically conditioned—at least in cats.

The principal drawback to the classical conditioning model, however, is that few patients recall any single event or trauma—nothing equivalent to that puff of air on the experimental cats—that caused the first panic attack. As the case histories in chapter 1 show, the attack that heralds the onset of panic disorder comes out of the blue.

The fear-of-fear principle presents another problem. The model makes it difficult to distinguish the signal for a panic attack from the symptoms of that same attack—something of an intellectual version of the chicken-or-egg problem. Dizziness, for example, could be either a signal that the patient learns to fear or a symptom that an attack has already begun. The same confusion between signal and symptom applies to sweaty palms, butterflies in the stomach, feelings of unreality, or any other sign of panic. Because of this confusion, it is difficult to say whether the patient fears fear, as the model proposes, or simply fears panic attacks, which is one of the diagnostic criteria of the disease.

What does it mean to call a theory of panic disorder sociological?

The sociological perspective derives somewhat from psychological ideas. The difference is that where psychology looks inward, at the often-hidden workings of the mind of a single individual, sociology focuses outward, analyzing the lives of large numbers of people for the common features in the social environment that influence their behavior.

What is the sociological explanation of panic disorder?

Sociological studies of panic disorder reveal a relationship between the disease and major life passages or crises. In a significant and large number of cases, panic disorder begins within a few months of a stressful event, such as a high school or college graduation, the loss of a spouse, or the birth of a child.

Does research support the sociological theory of panic disorder?

A considerable body of evidence indicates that in a great many cases panic disorder begins in the wake of a major life event.

For example, recent work on bereavement reveals that a small but significant number of people who experience the death of a close loved one react with depression and anxiety disorders, including panic. Some evidence indicates that this kind of reaction is particularly common among elderly people losing a spouse and among individuals whose spouse, child, or parent is killed in a sudden traumatic event like a car or airplane accident.

Depression following childbirth is well known and even expected. It is less well known that panic and other anxiety disorders are also more likely in the months after bringing a new child into the world. In women, these reactions may be both a physical response to the experience of pregnancy and birth and a mental reaction to their psychological and social lives. Stress, poor family and social support, and certain personality traits make anxiety reactions more likely.

Although men experience depression and anxiety disorders after birth in smaller numbers than women do, some new fathers go through similar psychological reactions. This fact shows how important the psychological and social setting of life change is to the development of diseases like panic disorder, as compared to the purely biological effects of the pregnancy and childbirth.

If the various theories explaining the origin of panic disorder are put together, what do they tell us?

It is almost certain that panic disorder comes from multiple causes, resulting not from one distinct source—the way a cold arises from infection by a specific virus—but from a number of complementary and contributing factors. As research continues, we will continue to learn more and understand these interactions better.

Assembling the current evidence yields this picture of the disease's beginnings:

Panic disorder is at least partly biological in origin. The disease, or a tendency to it, can be inherited. The affected physiological mechanisms involve specific areas of the brain, including the locus ceruleus; abnormalities in neurotransmitters, such as norepinephrine, serotonin, and GABA; receptor abnormalities, including the benzodiazepine receptors; and respiratory and acid-base dysfunction. Cardiac abnormalities may also have something to do with the disease.

Childhood experiences play a role in the development of panic disorder. Even if a tendency to the disease is inherited, that doesn't mean that an individual will necessarily develop panic disorder. A mentally ill or alcohol- or drug-dependent parent, sexual or physical abuse at an early age, and negative and dysfunctional parenting all make it more likely that the disease will emerge or develop later in life, particularly among people who have inherited a tendency to panic disorder.

Personality traits may be linked to panic disorder. Behavioral inhibition and separation anxiety—which may be the same personality structure seen from different perspectives—increase the risk of panic disorder.

The onset of panic disorder is associated with major passages in life. Panic disorder is most likely to arise in reaction to the stress of events that signal changes in life responsibilities—graduation, a big promotion at work, marriage or divorce, the birth of a child, or the sudden death of someone very close, for example.

We hear a lot these days about people causing their own illnesses from unhealthy lifestyles—cancer from smoking, heart disease from a high-fat diet, stroke from failure to exercise, for example. If I have panic disorder, is the disease my fault?

Absolutely and categorically not. Panic disorder results from a complex interaction of genetic inheritance, personality type, and psychological and social history. It isn't something you bring on yourself.

Too often our society sees anxiety, depression, panic, and similar psychiatric disorders as failures of the will. "Just do it," the ad commands. "When the going gets tough, the tough get going," the proverb dictates. Take such hard-nosed sentiments to heart, and you'll start thinking that the only thing wrong with someone who has panic disorder is an overdose of cowardice.

That's not the case, though. Panic disorder is a disease, not a failure of bravery. It needs to be treated as the serious illness that it is. And people with panic disorder need to understand that relief from the pain and suffering of their disease is possible and available.

Chapter Four

WHO CAN HELP ME WITH PANIC DISORDER?

I've been to doctor after doctor about symptoms that sound very much like panic attacks. I've been through all sorts of tests too. The doctors can't give me a diagnosis, and all the tests are negative. What's going on here?

Sadly, this experience with panic attack and panic disorder is all too common. It's frustrating, too, for both patient and physician.

As we saw in chapter 2, the symptoms of a panic attack can signal any of a long list of physical and mental diseases. Since most primary care physicians are not trained extensively in diagnosing psychiatric illness, and since most patients with panic disorder visit the doctor complaining of specific distress like chest pain or stomach upset rather than panic attack, the underlying disease is often missed.

This statement, from a patient subsequently diagnosed with panic disorder, illustrates how difficult the dilemma can be:

I went to [my family] doctor and he did a number of tests. He thought at first I had multiple sclerosis, but he ruled that out, finally, and said he wasn't sure what I had. So he sent me to a neurologist. The neurologist also did a number of tests and finally gave me a diagnosis of "nonspecific idiopathic neuropathy." I asked him what that was and he didn't give me much of an explanation. He just said that maybe I should see a psychiatrist.

People with panic disorder are high utilizers of medical services. One study found that patients with the disease had consulted up to ten physicians before their fundamental problem was diagnosed. Another research project revealed that the specialists most seen by panic disorder patients are otolaryngologists (ear, nose, and throat doctors), endocrinologists, neurologists, and urologists. The terrible truth is that, if you have panic disorder and you've already been through a number of doctors and dozens of expensive laboratory tests without reaching a final diagnosis, you're not alone.

Is panic disorder easy to diagnose?

It can be a tough call. Even though the disease has a clear-cut definition, it can be difficult to recognize in the hustle and bustle of a medical clinic that focuses on physical illnesses, not mental disorders. Unless the physician is aware of the possibility of psychiatric disease, he or she may overlook panic disorder in an attempt to alleviate the painful and distressing symptoms troubling the patient. And since many of panic disorder's signs mimic the symptoms of other diseases, both physical and psychiatric, diagnosis is doubly difficult.

Who is qualified to diagnose panic disorder?

All mental health professionals should be familiar enough with panic disorder to know what signs to look for and what questions to ask. Typically, psychiatrists (medical specialists in the diseases of the mind), psychologists (who receive extensive postgraduate clinical and academic training), and licensed clinical social workers (who also do postgraduate work in psychotherapy) can diagnose the condition.

All other things being equal, however, psychiatrists are the best qualified to deliver a definitive diagnosis of panic disorder and to treat the disease. Panic symptoms can be due to physical diseases and conditions, and psychiatrists are medical doctors well trained in sorting out the mental and physical contributions to an individual's complaints. Also, psychiatrists can prescribe medications, which are often useful in treating panic disorder.

The most qualified professional to determine the diagnosis of any mental disorder is a psychiatrist. Be assured that seeing a psychiatrist is not evidence that you are "crazy" or that you will soon be confined to a straitjacket in a padded room and locked up in the state mental hospital. Psychiatrists are simply specialists in the diseases of the mind, the professionals best qualified to determine the cause of your symptoms and initiate effective treatment.

Why can't I rely on my family physician to diagnose panic disorder?

Primary care physicians have to function as generalists who are familiar with a wide variety of diseases and problems—everything from ordinary orthopedic injuries like ankle sprains and tendinitis to common colds and herpes and serious chronic diseases like cancer and diabetes. Except for those few who have a particular personal interest in psychiatric medicine, primary care physicians are usually unlikely to have the knowledge and examination skills needed to diagnose mental illness.

It's a shame really. Various research studies indicate that as many as 30 to 40 percent of people visiting their doctors are seeing them for physical complaints with primary psychiatric causes. This happens a great deal with panic disorder, with its chest and stomach pains, respiratory distress, and numbness in feet and hands.

There's no doubt that psychiatric illnesses are under-diagnosed. Increasingly, psychiatrists and other mental health professionals are launching efforts to help primary care physicians learn more about mental disorders, recognize their symptoms, and know when to make appropriate referrals to psychiatrists. Currently, however, you shouldn't expect more from your primary care doctor than a referral to a psychiatrist combined with a sense of support for the pain you are suffering as a result of the disease.

What kind of training do psychiatrists undergo?

It is very extensive. After completing college, they must graduate from an accredited four-year medical school and complete at least four years of psychiatric residency. (Some psychiatric specialties require an extra year of training.) The first year of psychiatric residency consists largely of general psychiatry, internal medicine, pediatrics, and neurology. In the subsequent years of their training, psychiatric residents spend additional time in both inpatient hospitals and outpatient clinics, where they learn different approaches to treating mental diseases with medications, electroconvulsive therapy, psychotherapy, behavior therapy, family and marital therapy, child and adolescent therapy, and in some programs, sex therapy. During their residency, psychiatrists in training work in the emergency room handling crisis interventions, and they provide psychiatric consultations in medical units such as obstetrics and surgery.

Like all physicians, psychiatrists must pass exams to earn state licenses. To keep their licenses current, and to help ensure that they stay current with developments in this fast-changing field of medicine, they are required to complete a certain number of continuing education credits in psychiatry each year.

In comparison to psychiatrists, how are psychologists trained?

To begin with, psychologists are not medical doctors, so they do not prescribe medication, perform physical examinations, or order laboratory tests. Following graduation from college, they enter a graduate program, either at a university or at a stand-alone professional school, that leads to a doctoral degree. On average, psychologists spend seven years working on the doctorate, earning either a Sci.D. or a Ph.D. The Sci.D. indicates more of a clinical orientation in the training program; the Ph.D. is evidence of research-oriented training.

Following the doctorate, psychologists have to complete an internship in a hospital or organized health care setting and at least one year of supervised clinical work before they can practice on their own. Like psychiatrists, psychologists are licensed by the state and must complete continuing-education requirements in the field to keep their licenses current.

What do licensed clinical social workers and other therapists do, and how are they trained?

Licensed clinical social workers (L.C.S.W.'s) diagnose mental, emotional, and behavioral disorders and treat them with psychotherapy. They can work with individuals, families, and groups. L.C.S.W.'s have either a master's degree (M.S.W.) or a doctorate (D.S.W. or Ph.D.) in social work with a psychotherapeutic focus. They have also undergone a supervised internship and clinical training experiences that usually last three years.

L.C.S.W.'s are licensed by the state. They practice in a wide variety of settings, including hospitals, mental health clinics, schools, and community organizations.

A number of states also license therapists who have been through similar postgraduate programs, typically with an emphasis on psychology and psychotherapy rather than clinical social work. California, as one example, licenses marriage, family, and child counselors (M.F.C.C.'s), who have finished a master's degree in psychology, completed a supervised internship, and passed state-administered written and oral examinations. Other states license R.N.'s with additional training as therapists. In all states, members of the clergy can engage in pastoral counseling.

L.C.S.W.'s, M.F.C.C.'s, and similarly trained professionals typically charge less than either psychiatrists or psychologists. Because of their training, they look principally at the emotional issues in mental disorders, in contrast to psychiatrists, who follow a disease model and see panic disorder as a complex interplay of emotional, psychic, and physical factors.

How can I find a psychiatrist?

Unless you happen to know a psychiatrist as a personal friend or a business acquaintance, finding one may seem like a daunting, difficult, and demanding task. In truth, though, many resources are available to direct you to the right professional.

One place you don't want to go for a referral is the phone book. Except for providing the doctor's office address and phone number, the phone book offers little or no information on credentials, experience, or educational background.

Here are some better places to begin the search:

• *Your personal family doctor, internist, or gynecologist.* Tell your physician your symptoms, let him or her know why you think you may be suffering from panic disorder, and ask for a referral to a psychiatrist who is adept at handling the disease. Ideally, your doctor already knows you and your medical history well, can evaluate your symptoms and complaints, and will be able to tell you whether seeing a psychiatrist makes sense. He or she may perform necessary preliminary examinations and laboratory tests to rule out physical causes, such as hyperthyroidism, heart disease, or respiratory disease.

If you belong to an HMO, you will probably have to obtain a referral from your personal physician before seeing a psychiatrist. If you see a private physician rather than one in an HMO, get a copy of your medical records to take with you. The psychiatrist will want to look at them.

• *The psychiatry department at the nearest medical school.* The medical school or the hospital affiliated with it may operate a clinic that focuses on panic and other anxiety disorders. If not, you can ask for the names of professionals in your area who know how to work with panic disorder.

• *The physician referral service at your local hospital.* Some hospitals have a mental health program; even if they don't, they can give you the names of psychiatrists along with their educational backgrounds, credentials, and professional affiliations. Be aware, however, that hospitals refer only to physicians on their own staffs.

• *The physician referral service or community outreach department of a private psychiatric hospital.* Here again you will receive only the names of staff members. Still, because of its experience and expertise with mental disease, a psychiatric hospital has a good understanding of the treatment needs of panic disorder and can make an appropriate referral.

• *Your employer's employee assistance program (EAP).* Originally set up to help employees with alcohol and drug abuse, EAPs have broadened their scope to include a wide variety of emotional and mental disorders that undercut employee effectiveness. EAP providers are trained in crisis intervention, and they can make referrals as necessary. EAP programs are designed to protect an employee's privacy, but there is always the risk that coworkers or superiors will find out that you are seeking assistance. Still, if you have had panic attacks at work, your employer may urge you to consult with the EAP.

• *A community mental health clinic.* Supported by tax revenues, such clinics provide mental health services on a sliding scale of fees—the more money you make, the more you pay. Accessibility and level of service vary from state to state, even county to county. Call your local health department, state health department, or state human services bureau for information.

• *A religious mental health center.* Groups like Jewish Family Service and Catholic Family Service offer mental health services, usually provided by clinical social workers. Psychologists and psychiatrists may also be on staff, or referrals to outside professionals can be made.

• *A priest, rabbi, or minister.* Most members of the clergy study psychology in seminary, and many have had extensive training in pastoral counseling and spiritual direction. In some states, in fact, clerical degrees, such as the M.Div. and D.Min., can serve as the basis for mental health licensing. While panic disorder usually requires more treatment than a member of the clergy is able to provide, he or she can be supportive and direct you to a suitable professional.

• *A friend or relative who has been treated successfully for panic disorder.* Since panic disorder often runs in families, you may well have a close relative who has suffered from the disease and overcome it. It's also possible that you have a friend with panic or another anxiety disorder. Ask the friend or relative for the name of the physician who provided treatment. If your friend or family member lives at a distance, ask his or her doctor for a referral to a psychiatrist close by.

Be aware, however, that working with the same psychiatrist as a first-degree relative or a close friend can pose problems. The doctor may already know something about you from work with his or her prior patient and thus has lost objectivity. Some professionals refuse to treat members of the same family, while others do it routinely. If you see a psychiatrist who has also worked with a family member or friend, discuss the issue openly. Be sure that you feel comfortable about proceeding with the therapeutic relationship.

• *A self-help or patient-support group.* The appendix lists a number of organizations that can guide you to support groups for people with anxiety disorders. Contact the group, locate a group meeting near you, and show up. It is likely that people in the group know which psychiatrists are good at diagnosing and treating panic disorder. You may also be able to locate a support group through your local hospital's community outreach department.

• *A student health center.* Many colleges and universities and some professional schools provide free or low-cost health care on campus. Ask a physician or social worker for a referral to a psychiatrist.

• *Local reference books and magazines.* Regional publishers assemble health care guides that list the best doctors in a region or large metropolitan area. Examples are *The 1997 Guide to Good Health* published by *Philadelphia* magazine, *The Best Doctors in the New York Metropolitan Area* (1997), and *The Best Doctors in America—Northeast Edition* (1997). City and state magazines often run regular features naming the top medical professionals, including psychiatrists, in the area. An example is the April 1996 issue of *New Jersey Monthly* entitled "Top Docs." Your local reference librarian should be able to direct you to the correct regional guides and magazine issues.

• *The American Psychiatric Association (APA).* Contact the district branch of the APA, the principal professional organization for psychiatrists, to ask for the names of qualified specialists in your area. Phone numbers, e-mail addresses, street addresses, and contact names for APA district branches in the United States, Puerto Rico, and Canada appear in the appendix.

How do I know whether a particular psychiatrist is competent to handle my symptoms?

One way to ensure that you are dealing with a psychiatrist whose training meets a high standard of competence is to seek one whose credentials include certification by the American Board of Psychiatry and Neurology (ABPN). ABPN certification is a sign of strong clinical competence, not excellence.

The ABPN was founded in 1934 to serve the public interest by certifying psychiatrists and neurologists who have met rigorous criteria of preparation and examination. The nonprofit ABPN is one of the certifying boards making up the American Board of Medical Specialties.

Earning certification by the ABPN requires the physician to have achieved these educational, practice, and testing benchmarks:

- Education
  - The physician must have an M.D. (doctor of medicine) or D.O. (doctor of osteopathy) degree from an accredited school of medicine or osteopathy. Medical graduates from foreign countries must have an equivalent degree.
  - Following medical school, the doctor must complete at least four years of postgraduate training, of which no less than three must be in psychiatry. Some subspecialties in psychiatry require five years of study.
- Practice
  - An unlimited license to practice in the United States is required.
  - Personal and professional conduct must meet the highest standard.
- Examinations
  - The physician must pass a day-long written test covering the basic, clinical, and psychiatric sciences.
  - To demonstrate good clinical skills, the physician has to pass an oral test that includes taking a his-

tory and doing a preliminary examination of a patient. The psychiatrist also watches a videotape of a patient being interviewed and answers questions from the examiners about the patient's condition.

Obviously, these requirements are rigorous and extensive. Any psychiatrist who has met them is competent on a professional basis to handle the diagnosis and treatment of mental illness, including panic disorder.

Beyond board certification, psychiatrists can become fellows of the ABPN by making a special contribution to the field.

The words *board-certified* often appear after a psychiatrist's name in the phone book. Do they mean that this doctor is certified by the American Board of Psychiatry and Neurology?

Not necessarily. Other certifying boards exist that are not members of the American Board of Medical Specialties and that typically set lower standards of qualification. It is best to ensure that any psychiatrist you consult with is indeed certified by the ABPN. Information about certification is available from such referral sources as the county medical society, a university medical school, or the American Psychiatric Association.

How can I be sure that the psychiatrist I am talking to has the necessary skills to handle my problem?

In evaluating a psychiatrist, medical school is less important than residency training. Medical schools all teach the same curriculum, but residencies vary, often substantially, from program to program. Feel free to ask any doctor you visit where he or she did residency training and what the orientation of the program was. Some programs emphasize psychopharmacology—using medications to treat mental illness and managing the psychiatric disorders that occur in physically ill patients—while others focus on psychotherapy, or talk therapy. Yet others teach both. Programs change over time too.

Unsurprisingly, the residency program an individual psychiatrist went through often strongly influences the way he or she practices the specialty. If you don't like the idea of taking medication, look for a psychiatrist who trained in a psychotherapeutically oriented program. But if you are uncomfortable with talk therapy, seek a psychopharmacologically trained psychiatrist.

You can find out about a psychiatrist's residency by asking him or her directly, inquiring with the local mental health association or the district branch of the American Psychiatric Association, or checking with the referring physician or other professional. The *APA Biographical Directory* gives a profile of each member psychiatrist of the American Psychiatric Association and lists his or her training, experience, and interests. Released most recently in 1986, the directory is now undergoing revision, and an updated edition should be available soon.

Should I seek a professional who specializes in panic disorder?

It will obviously be of benefit to you to work with a professional who has experience with the disease. While panic disorder is common—one out of three adults experiences panic attacks in a given year, and panic disorder affects two to six percent of the general population—the disease is such a mimic of various physical and mental disorders that it can severely test diagnostic and therapeutic skills.

Here are some questions you can ask to assess a psychiatrist's understanding of and expertise in panic disorder:

• *"What percentage of your practice does panic disorder represent?"* It's unlikely that a psychiatrist will specialize solely in panic disorder. Still, a professional with a practice that is 20 percent panic disorder will feel much more comfortable handling the disease than someone who rarely treats the disease.

• *"Do you teach, write, or lecture about panic disorder?"* Talks about panic disorder to community groups like service clubs or churches, a clinical appointment at a medical school, or medical journal publications all indicate a special interest in the disease and up-to-date knowledge about it.

• *"Have you trained specifically in panic disorder or related diseases?"* This question goes back to the psychiatrist's residency and any subsequent professional training he or she may have had.

• *"Do you receive many referrals from other doctors for patients with panic disorder?"* The more referrals, the more primary care doctors recognize this psychiatrist as an expert in the disease.

Panic disorder has been recognized as a separate disease only in the past twenty years. Some of the most effective treatments have been developed recently. How can I tell whether a psychiatrist understands the state of the art in treating the disease?

If you live close to a medical school, the best evidence that a psychiatrist is keeping up with the times is an academic appointment at the medical school as a lecturer, assistant professor, associate professor, or—rarely—full professor.

Many of these clinical appointments are unpaid positions that require the physician to spend about a half-day per week teaching medical students and residents and attending what are called grand rounds—a major lecture on a medical topic or a conference where cases are discussed. Academic service demands that a psychiatrist stay current on research into diagnosis and treatment methods.

Another indication is affiliation with a hospital that is well respected in the community. This position gives the psychiatrist the opportunity to exchange news and ideas with peers and remain up-to-date.

Don't be shy about asking a psychiatrist for his or her academic or hospital affiliations. Such questions show you've done your homework and know what you're looking for.

I would feel comfortable working only with a psychiatrist who shares my gender, age, and cultural background. Is it okay to specify what I want when I am looking for referrals?

Absolutely. It is very important that you feel comfortable working with any psychiatrist. If gender, age, and cultural background matter to you, say so when you are asking for referrals.

Will my health insurance cover psychiatric care?

With the rise of managed care over the past several years, more and more insurers have cut back on the amount of mental health coverage they provide. Check your policy before you see a psychiatrist for the first time. It's better to know where you stand financially in advance of beginning treatment.

If it happens that your health insurance policy offers

only limited mental health coverage, find out from your employee representative at work whether other policies are available for you to choose from. It may be possible for you to change over to a plan with superior mental health benefits.

When I go to see a psychiatrist for the first time, what will happen?

Like any physician, the psychiatrist will want to know why you think you need treatment. He or she will also be interested in finding out more about your background, family, personal habits, and general health, including the approximate date of your most recent complete physical examination, and in reviewing your medical records. If it's been a while since you've had a physical, the psychiatrist will probably perform such an exam or refer you to your own physician or another doctor for necessary tests. As a medical doctor, a psychiatrist is qualified to interpret laboratory findings.

During this initial visit you should feel free to ask questions about fees, appointment flexibility, cancellation policy, and the processing of insurance forms. And be aware of how you react to the psychiatrist as an individual. A positive response is an important foundation for successful treatment.

How important are my personal reactions in selecting a psychiatrist?

They are extremely important. Indeed, the personal side of your reaction to a psychiatrist is every bit as significant as his or her professional qualifications. Therapy requires openness and trust between patient and physician. Obviously, that can happen only if you feel comfortable working with a given physician. Choosing a psychiatrist is something on the order of making a new friend; likes and dislikes count.

In the process of looking for referrals, collect the names of two to four possibilities. When you see the first psychiatrist on your list, do an emotional gut check. In addition to good training, current knowledge, and demonstrated clinical competence, you are looking for the right chemistry—a match between your personality style and the psychiatrist's. Ask yourself whether you like the prospect of working with this doctor for the next several weeks or months. How does it feel to talk about difficult problems with someone you've never met before? Does he or she pay attention to what you are saying and have a sense for your feelings? Was the doctor on time for your appointment, and was he or she interested in what you had to say? Is this a person you feel you can trust? If you suffer difficulties at night or on the weekends, will the psychiatrist be available to you even at odd hours? How do you like the office and the location—is it comfortable, convenient, and reassuring, or out-of-the-way, cold, and intimidating?

If something about the psychiatrist or the setting feels wrong or negative, go on to the next physician on your list. Should you go through four professionals without finding one who seems right, the problem may lie with you. Ask yourself whether you're really looking to find help, or if you're trying to avoid the issue.

How is a panic disorder diagnosis made?

Mental health professionals follow the diagnostic criteria set down in the fourth edition (1994) of the *Diagnostic and Statistical Manual of Mental Diseases*, which is published by the American Psychiatric Association and is commonly abbreviated as DSM-IV. The DSM-IV diagnosis of panic disorder has four key elements:

- Both of the following conditions must be true:
  - Panic attacks are repeated and unexpected.
  - At least one attack has been followed by a month or more of concern about future attacks, worry about the implications and consequences of panic attacks, or significant changes in behavior related to the attacks.
- Presence or absence of agoraphobia.
- Panic attacks are not due to a general medical condition nor to a substance, chemical, or medication.
- Panic attacks do not result from a psychiatric condition other than panic disorder.

Medical diagnosis begins by deciding not what a disease is but what it isn't—what physicians call rule-out's. Panic disorder is no different from any other disease in this regard. The doctor begins by making sure that the panic attack isn't the result of a general medical condition, medication, or another psychiatric disorder.

How will a psychiatrist decide whether or not a general medical condition or a medication is causing the panic attacks?

Every evaluation starts with a careful medical history that explores your background, any diseases or predispositions you may have inherited from your family, and your lifestyle and habits. For example, the premature deaths of one or both of your parents from cardiovascular disease gives a physician reason to investigate your cardiac health. And your doctor will want to know about the medications you have used or are taking and your use of alcohol and drugs, both now and in the past. Honesty, even about closeted family matters and illegal drug use, is in your own best interest. Remember: Your psychiatrist is trained to understand and work with exactly these issues.

The next step is a thorough physical examination, usually by your personal doctor, who will report back to the psychiatrist. The physician will be looking for signs of any medical condition that could bring on panic attacks. Chapter 2 discusses the physical conditions and diseases that can cause panic attacks. The physician will be looking for abnormalities such as enlarged thyroid or certain heart sounds that could indicate mitral valve prolapse. Depending on the findings from the physical examination and the medical history, the doctor may order various laboratory tests. Here are some of the common ones:

- An electrocardiogram (EKG or ECG) examines the electrical current produced by the contraction of the heart muscle and is useful in assessing cardiac health. An EKG is a likely test in the event of chest pain during panic attacks.

- An electroencephalogram (EEG) measures the electrical activity of brain cells through electrodes placed on the scalp. It can be used in diagnosing neurological diseases. An EEG may be ordered for patients who have symptoms like vertigo or numbness on the feet and hands during an attack.

- A chest X ray can identify conditions in the lungs that may lead to the respiratory distress that often occurs in panic attacks.

- A chemical screen of the blood identifies electrolyte (sodium, potassium, and calcium) levels. This can be important in panic disorder since electrolyte imbalance is one of the possible physical causes of attacks.

- Blood tests can also be run to assess liver function and to determine whether the thyroid is over- or underactive. Again, liver and thyroid dysfunction may cause panic symptoms.

Once all the examinations are done and the lab results are in, the physician reviews the accumulated data and reaches what is called a differential diagnosis. That is, by ruling out some causes, the physician can reduce the number of possibilities, ideally leaving only one. For example, a normal EKG indicates no mitral valve prolapse; blood tests for electrolytes and thyroid hormones are normal; chest X ray is negative for pulmonary abnormality; and the patient reports no vertigo, dizziness, or tingling in the extremities during panic attacks, making an EEG unnecessary. In this case, the differential physical diagnosis would point toward panic disorder as the cause of the attacks.

Let's assume that the medical evaluation turns up no cause for the panic attacks. What happens next?

The next issue to be decided is whether the panic attacks come from some psychiatric condition other than panic disorder. As we saw in chapter 2, panic attacks have the same symptoms no matter which disorder causes them, and they can occur in practically any psychiatric illness.

How is panic disorder distinguished from other psychiatric illnesses?

The most telling difference between panic disorder and other diseases of the mind is the nature of the panic attacks and the patient's reaction to them. Remember: The symptoms of panic attack are precisely the same, no matter what the cause of the attack.

In panic disorder, panic attacks have to be repeated; one attack by itself is not a sign of the disease. At least some of the attacks must come out of the blue, with no identifiable trigger or cue. In addition, patients with panic disorder are concerned, worried, and even obsessed about the possibility of future attacks, often to the point where they alter their lives in an attempt—always ultimately ineffective—to avoid such distressing episodes.

A number of diseases related to panic disorder also lead commonly to panic attacks. The following descriptions of these maladies show how they differ from panic disorder, particularly in the specific sorts of cues that trigger the attacks:

- In social phobia, panic attacks result from exposure to situations in which one is watched or judged by large groups of people. Extreme panic reactions to speaking in public are a common example of social phobia.

- Specific phobia is cued by a particular object or being. Dogs, snakes, and spiders are typical triggers. The widespread and aptly named "fear of flying" is a specific phobia as well.

- A panic attack in obsessive-compulsive disorder (OCD) is set off by exposure to the object of the patient's obsession. For example, infection is a common obsession of people with OCD. Just the thought of being in the same room as a person with AIDS might initiate a panic attack in an OCD patient with an infection obsession.

- Panic arises in post-traumatic stress disorder when

the patient is exposed to an object, event, or situation that recalls the original trauma. A veteran who endured horrific battlefield experiences in Vietnam may launch into panic on hearing the *whump-whump-whump* of a helicopter overhead or hit the ground and break into a cold sweat in reaction to a car's backfire.

In contrast to these psychiatric diseases, panic disorder's attacks seem to come from nowhere, without a specific trigger or cue—no snakes, backfires, or elbow-rubbing with HIV-positive people.

I've experienced panic attacks, but I don't have any fear of going out in public. Does that mean that my panic attacks are the result of something other than panic disorder?

Not necessarily. Agoraphobia—the fear of public places—commonly occurs in conjunction with panic disorder, but the disease may also arise without it. As a result, the presence or absence of agoraphobia does not define panic disorder. However, recent research indicates that panic disorder with agoraphobia is the more severe form of the disease.

What are the diagnostic signs of agoraphobia?

There are three:

• The patient feels pronounced anxiety and fear about being in a wide variety of places or situations that are difficult or embarrassing to escape or where help may not be available in the event of a panic attack or panic symptoms.

- The patient avoids these situations, endures them only with great distress, or requires the presence of a companion.
- No other mental disorder accounts for the anxiety or avoidant behavior.

Can agoraphobialike anxiety arise in diseases other than panic disorder?

People with other mental disorders often develop avoidant anxiety and behavior based on their disease. What sets such fear off from agoraphobia—with its generalized fear of all spaces and places where escape is difficult or embarrassing—is the specific focus of the anxiety and the avoidance. For example, someone with a social phobia about public speaking may steer well clear of podiums, auditoriums, and church pulpits. A patient with a specific phobia about flying may avoid airports and reruns of *Memphis Belle*, yet be perfectly content on Amtrak or the subway. Similarly, a Vietnam War veteran with post-traumatic stress disorder triggered by helicopter sounds avoids those aircraft, yet comfortably flies on a jumbo jet to visit his family across the country.

In agoraphobia, by contrast, the fear is generalized to clusters of similar situations and places—such as all mass transit vehicles, bridges or tunnels everywhere and anywhere, and every sort of public gathering place, from shopping malls to Madison Square Garden. Agoraphobia is set apart by its general and nonspecific anxiety.

Can agoraphobia occur all by itself, without panic disorder?

Yes, it can. The difference between agoraphobia alone and panic disorder with agoraphobia is the panic attacks themselves. One of the distinguishing features of panic disorder is the degree of panic. In addition to the intense fear and anxiety that come on suddenly and hit a peak within about ten minutes, a panic attack also entails at least four of the following thirteen symptoms:

1. palpitations, pounding heart, or accelerated heart rate
2. sweating
3. trembling or shaking
4. sensations of short breath or smothering
5. feelings of choking
6. chest pain or discomfort
7. nausea or abdominal stress
8. feeling dizzy, unsteady, light-headed, or faint
9. feelings of unreality ("This seems like a dream") or depersonalization ("It felt like it was happening to someone else")
10. fear of losing control or going crazy
11. fear of dying (often from stroke or heart attack)
12. numbness or tingling, usually in the hands or feet
13. chills or hot flashes

A patient with agoraphobia alone experiences less than full-blown panic, what physicians call a limited-symptom attack. Usually someone with only agoraphobia focuses the anxiety on a single uncomfortable or distressing symptom, like losing bowel or bladder control, rather than on the complete range of panic attack symptoms.

If I suffer from panic disorder, is it likely to be the only disease I need to be concerned about?

Panic disorder is often complicated by other symptoms, conditions, and diseases. On the physical side of the ledger, patients with panic disorder commonly suffer from migraines, asthma, irritable bowel syndrome, and similar complaints. They may also be at heightened risk for hypertension and cardiovascular disease over a sustained period of time. Diagnostic work on panic disorder needs to assess the patient for these and related conditions, which can seriously affect the quality and quantity of life.

In the psychiatric column, major depression is the most common companion of panic disorder, affecting 40 to 80 percent of patients. Substance abuse is less common, but significant, appearing in a little more than one out of six people with the disease. If major depression or substance abuse is present along with panic disorder, all three diagnoses need to be made and treatment shaped accordingly.

Even though I've been having panic attacks and I'm afraid of having more of them, I feel an even greater discomfort at the idea of seeing a psychiatrist. What happens if I just bide my time and let the disease run its course?

That's almost certainly a bad idea. In some cases, panic attacks disappear on their own, or they lessen in severity. But spontaneous disappearance isn't something you can count on. In many cases, panic attacks continue for years, possibly for the rest of your life. And the disease can actually get worse.

You also need to be aware of the consequences of untreated panic disorder over time. People who suffer from panic attacks have a high degree of functional impairment—that is, they have a hard time holding a job, advancing their careers, and pulling their weight in marriage and family. Some people are so impaired they can't leave their homes. Panic disorder brings with it a greatly increased risk of drug or alcohol addiction, marital breakup, suicide attempt, clinical depression, and financial dependence.

Doing nothing about panic attacks is simply and purely unwise. In 90 percent of cases, the disease can be treated successfully. Without that treatment, however, people with panic disorder face a declining quality of life and the prospect of premature death, possibly by suicide or from complications of the disease. While psychiatric treatment may seem scary at the moment, just waiting around for panic disorder to go away on its own will prove a good deal more frightening in the end.

Chapter Five

WHAT HAPPENS
IN PSYCHOTHERAPY?

To begin with, what exactly is psychotherapy?

The word *psychotherapy* comes from two Greek roots that mean "treating the mind." That's precisely what psychotherapy is—the application of psychological techniques to alleviate the symptoms and treat the causes of mental disorders.

There's nothing mysterious about psychotherapy. It's a proven, effective way of dealing with diseases of the mind.

Psychotherapy is sometimes called "talk therapy" to distinguish it from therapies that treat mental disorders with medications. Talking is indeed part of psychotherapy. In a psychotherapy session you discuss your symptoms, behaviors, problems, and feelings with the psychotherapist, who listens carefully and provides feedback. Depending on the kind of psychotherapy you are doing, the focus of the work may be on present issues in your life, or you and your psychotherapist may explore critical areas of childhood as key experiences in your emotional evolution. The psychotherapist uses his or her long training in human behavior and psychological processes to uncover material that can help you understand your own problems. The psychotherapist's thoughtful questions and empathic observations can increase your self-knowledge, helping you identify negative patterns and changing them into positive assets.

I've been through career counseling. Isn't psychotherapy pretty much the same thing?

Only superficially. The point of career counseling is to present you with a path to follow or a choice of paths to select among. In career counseling, you are working with an expert to help you chart your way through a difficult or complicated process, such as taking the next step in your education or career. Career counseling focuses on educational or vocational goals, not on psychological issues. The counselor talks more than you do, presenting information, guidelines, resources, even emotional support. Career counseling puts the main responsibility on the counselor.

Psychotherapy lays much more weight on the work done by the patient. A psychotherapist doesn't preach. Instead, he or she helps you see the recurrent patterns of thoughts and feelings and understand how they influence your life. It's up to you to make up your mind to take charge and fix what you can. Psychotherapy offers a forum for self-discovery, insight, and emotional change.

Ideally, the relationship between you and a psychotherapist is deeper, more complicated, and more productive than it would be with a career counselor. The relationship with a psychotherapist is built on two important cornerstones.

Therapeutic alliance. It's something like a good working relationship—the rational, conscious, healthy part of you forms a relationship with those same parts in your psychotherapist. The relationship is based on an agreement between you and the psychotherapist that the two of you will work together toward a goal—an improvement in your psychological condition.

The therapeutic alliance gives the psychotherapist space to make specific suggestions and offer insights to the patient. And it allows the patient to listen to these ideas even if they arouse hostile, negative, or angry feelings. The therapeutic alliance removes barriers to insight and provides a foundation for effective treatment.

Consider, for example, a patient whose panic disorder is rooted in traumatic separation experiences as a child growing up with an alcoholic parent. Like many adult children of alcoholics, this patient is so wrapped in denial that he or she hates to admit that the parent was an alcoholic and never even thinks the word, much less says it out loud. In a therapy session, in which the patient described a long weekend the parent had lost to a case of whiskey, the therapist offers an insight, such as "Wouldn't you consider a three-day blackout a clear-cut sign of alcoholism?" Immediately, the patient reacts angrily, thinking something along the lines of "Don't call my parent an alcoholic!" The anger could tear apart an ordinary relationship between friends. Yet in the psychotherapeutic setting, the therapeutic alliance allows the relationship to go on, and even deepen, despite the negative feelings. The therapeutic alliance is the key that lets the patient to take in difficult information and grow from it.

Transference. In psychotherapy, feelings associated with significant people from the patient's past shift unconsciously onto a person in the present—namely, the psychotherapist. Let's use the patient with an alcoholic parent as the example again. Because the patient was often intoxicated and emotionally unavailable, the patient as a child developed powerful feelings of fear and powerlessness, as well as anger and resentment over the parent's emotional abandonment. Because these feeling were unacceptable, the patient has repressed them, burying the emotions deep within the unconscious mind. As the patient starts to become aware of how much has been repressed, these feelings emerge in the psychotherapy session. Completely unconsciously, the patient experiences the psychotherapist as if he or she were the inconsistent, unavailable parent from decades past. The very feelings of anger, resentment, fear, and powerlessness that arose toward the parent back then now emerge toward the psychotherapist. In a very real way, the patient is dealing with the psychotherapist as if he or she were the parent.

The difference is that the psychotherapist doesn't respond as the parent used to. Instead of further abandoning the child, the psychotherapist listens to the anger the patient expresses and reflects, "Can you see that's just how you felt during those long confusing weekends? You must have been terribly frightened and anxious."

Transference pays two important benefits in this kind of interaction. It brings to the surface feelings the patient was unaware of, deepening self-understanding. And the patient discovers that people don't always behave as the parent once did, by further abandoning the child. The therapist remains connected with the patient and offers insight and support. Transference is both cathartic—that is, revealing unresolved feelings through emotional outburst and cleansing—and therapeutic—that is, helping to resolve and treat the now-revealed feelings.

How long has psychotherapy been in use?

Ever since there have been humans, we have sought out others with special knowledge, insight, and empathy to help us solve personal problems and uncover the psychological sources of pain and suffering. In primitive cultures, for example, elders served as repositories of traditional knowledge about the mind and its workings. Various religious traditions foster psychotherapylike practices and relationships. For example, Christian monks and clerics since the Middle Ages have studied what is called spiritual direction—an organized approach to the development of the deep self, in which a spiritual adept works with a novice—that resembles aspects of psychotherapy.

Psychotherapy in its contemporary form is dated to 1895, when Josef Breuer, an Austrian physician who collaborated with Sigmund Freud, used talk therapy to treat a woman with a phobia about drinking water from a glass. Breuer's observations about his work with this and similar cases prompted much of Freud's thinking and led to the development of the modern forms of psychotherapy.

Is there only one type of psychotherapy?

Many schools of psychotherapy are currently in practice in the United States. The following list names the types that have been used frequently for panic disorder and researched most deeply:

- classical psychoanalysis
- psychodynamic psychotherapy (traditional and brief, as well as panic-focused)
- supportive psychotherapy
- cognitive-behavioral psychotherapy

What is classical psychoanalysis?

It is the approach to understanding human personality originated by Sigmund Freud (1856–1939). An Austrian neurologist, Freud devoted his career to exploring the human psyche and wrote books, like *Ego and Id* and *Civilization and Its Discontents*, that are considered key texts in modern intellectual history.

In the decades since Freud's death, psychoanalysts have altered, modified, and added to his ideas. Karen Horney, Erich Fromm, Erik Erikson, and Harry Stack Sullivan are some of the psychotherapists who developed their own interpretations of, and approaches to, psychoanalysis.

Classical psychoanalysis is the oldest form of psychotherapy, and it is the one that entails the least interaction between you and the psychotherapist. The therapist sits out of sight of the patient, who often lies on a couch. The therapist says little and often is completely silent. Psychotherapy sessions consist mostly of you talking about emotional experiences from childhood, typically by free association—essentially saying the first thing that comes to mind and following wherever it leads—and recounting dreams. Transference is key to psychoanalysis, as you move repressed feelings from childhood out of the unconscious and onto the psychotherapist. Ideally, psychoanalysis uncovers deeply hidden and repressed feelings from the past and helps you see how they influence seemingly unrelated actions, behaviors, and emotions in the present.

The advantage of psychoanalysis is that it permits a deep and detailed look at your psychic makeup. It is an excellent choice for people who want to understand themselves in exquisite detail, particularly with an eye to restructuring their personalities.

The disadvantage to psychoanalysis, particularly in its pure form, is that it is extremely time-consuming and very slow in producing results. Psychoanalysts meet with patients as often as five times a week, sometimes for periods of five to even ten years. Since psycho-analysts charge by the session, the total cost can be stag-gering. And because this approach unfolds over time, psychoanalysis alleviates disturbing symptoms slowly.

Is classical analysis effective against panic disorder?

It should be, particularly for patients with disease rooted in deeply repressed and emotionally charged childhood experiences. People who grew up in compli-cated families with severe psychological dysfunction would likely profit from the in-depth look at themselves that psychoanalysis can provide.

The drawback to psychoanalysis is the lengthy time and tremendous expense it requires. Additionally, psychoanalysis provides little relief from symptoms, at least over the short term. Since panic disorder is so frightening and disabling to the person who suffers from it, and since psychoanalysis offers little prospect for improvement in less than several years, it is a poor choice for treating the disease.

What is psychodynamic psychotherapy?

This approach is rooted in psychoanalysis, in that it also deals with exposing unconscious childhood experiences through transference. The main difference is that the psychotherapist and the patient sit face to face, allow-ing more direct interaction. Traditional psychodynamic psychotherapy examines personality patterns that are related to the development of panic disorder.

Another form of this approach is called brief psychodynamic psychotherapy. It takes less time to complete by limiting the focus of the process to specific goals and outcomes rather than a broad, detailed exploration of personality.

Does psychodynamic psychotherapy work against panic disorder?

The advantage of traditional psychodynamic psychotherapy over classical psychoanalysis is that it accomplishes a similarly deep exploration, but often more quickly. Still it can be time-consuming because it casts a wide net.

A recently developed form of psychodynamic psychotherapy that focuses on panic—and called, unsurprisingly, panic-focused psychodynamic psychotherapy (PFPP)—offers one of the most exciting new prospects for treatment of the disease. Developed by Fredric Busch, M.D., Arnold Cooper, M.D., Barbara Milrod, M.D., and Theodore Shapiro, M.D., of the Cornell University Medical College, panic-focused psychodynamic psychotherapy has delivered important clinical results. PFPP is the newest psychotherapeutic approach to panic disorder and therefore the least studied.

What is panic-focused psychodynamic psychotherapy based on, and how does it proceed?

The core understanding of PFPP is that people with panic disorder share particular psychological factors that predispose them to the disease. These factors include personality problems, difficulties with certain kinds of emotional experiences, and unconscious conflicts about separation, anger, and sexuality. In many cases, these factors contribute to making the person unassertive, insecure, and dependent.

Research conducted by the formulators of PFPP showed that clearly stressful events precede the onset of panic disorder. In most patients, this event consists of increased responsibilities—the beginning of a big research project, adding a child to the family, or promotion into a major administrative position, for example. The patient's mind links this event to a frightening childhood experience, in which the individual felt rage at rejection by a parent. Fearful that this rage could destroy the parent—an illusion typical of children—the child actually became more dependent upon the mother or father. This created a paradoxical cycle of emotion in which rage and dependence fed off each other. The child was filled with anger at the parent yet, because of the anger, needed the parent even more, which further built the anger. In adulthood the same cycle of emotion is set off by a stressful event, such as a job promotion. The emotions become overwhelming, and panic is the result.

Instead of examining the entire personality of the individual, PFPP emphasizes the panic, any agoraphobia, and the dynamics that lie behind them. The goal of the therapy is to alleviate panic symptoms, prevent relapse following psychotherapy, and restore the person's ability to function normally.

There are three phases to PFPP. The objective of the first is to explore and relieve panic symptoms. The psychotherapist delves with you into the life event that precipitated the panic attacks and the feelings surrounding it. As this exploration deepens, the psychotherapist obtains a view of the psychological dynamics that led to the onset of panic. Often he or she can help you understand more about conflicts surrounding separation and independence, recognizing and managing anger and, in some cases, disquieting sexual feelings.

Initially, these conflicts lie in the unconscious, outside your awareness. As the psychotherapy proceeds, the conflicts enter conscious awareness and you begin to understand them.

The second phase of the treatment goes even deeper, as a way of reducing your vulnerability to the return of panic attacks. Typically transference onto the psychotherapist heightens, making it easier to further uncover and unravel the unconscious conflicts that fed into the panic episodes. Working these issues through can help you feel more assertive and less anxious over separation, anger, and sexual concerns.

In PFPP's final phase, the experience of terminating treatment allows a look at your difficulties with separation and anger—issues that arise naturally in the course of ending the relationship with the psychotherapist. Voicing these feelings and understanding them in the context of the psychotherapeutic relationship makes them appear less frightening to you. Sometimes revisiting these emotions causes a temporary return of the symptoms. Still, this phase of treatment gives you a new understanding of, and ability to tolerate, separation and loss.

Does PFPP treat panic disorder successfully?

As of yet, no large-scale study has compared PFPP with other psychotherapeutic approaches to panic disorder. The clinical evidence to date, however, indicates that PFPP not only works over the short term—that is, alleviating symptoms by the time the patient leaves psychotherapy—but also has a good record in keeping patients symptom-free for longer periods and preventing relapse. The final word isn't in, but there's every reason to believe that PFPP is a good choice for panic disorder treatment. It's especially useful for individuals troubled by self-esteem and relationship problems before panic disorder began.

PFPP offers some of the same benefits of deep insight into one's psychological nature as classical psycho-therapy. What makes it superior for panic disorder is its clear focus on panic symptoms and its ability to provide relief much more quickly and at a lower cost.

What is supportive psychotherapy?

This is the form of psychotherapy that comes closest to counseling. Focusing on the here-and-now rather than emotional events in childhood, the psychotherapist pro-vides advice, guidance, and direction. Instead of waiting for you to become aware of a pattern on your own and do something about it, the supportive psychotherapist says, "Here's what's happening. Now I'm going to show you the right action to take."

Supportive psychotherapy works in a direction op-posite to classical psychoanalysis and PFPP. Those two approaches take you back into emotional patterns that originated in childhood, by helping you break down de-fense mechanisms against your feelings. Supportive psychotherapy stays in the present, and it bolsters de-fense mechanisms as a tried and true way of coping with current turmoil and stress.

Supportive psychotherapy doesn't offer the deep in-sights available through classical psychotherapy and PFPP. It's about fixing what's broken through explana-tion and encouragement.

Supportive psychotherapy can last from several weeks to several months depending on the extent of your psychological problems and the severity of your symptoms. It tends to be used principally by clinical psychologists, licensed clinical social workers, and marriage and family therapists, but psychiatrists also incorporate supportive-psychotherapeutic techniques into their work with patients who can benefit from them.

Does supportive psychotherapy work against panic disorder?

Used all by itself, supportive psychotherapy is generally insufficient. However, it works well in combination with medication, which will be discussed in detail in chapter 6. The medication alleviates symptoms and provides a quiet psychological space to make use of the counseling and education provided by supportive psychotherapy.

What is cognitive-behavioral psychotherapy?

It is a combination of insights and approaches originated in two different but related schools of psychotherapy: behavioral and cognitive.

Behavioral psychotherapy has been in practice since the 1950s, originating largely in the work of psychologist B. F. Skinner. From the perspective of behavioral psychotherapy, panic attacks are a learned response to a feared stimulus. A behavioral psychotherapist works with the patient to help unlearn the physical reactions that lead to panic attacks. One way is to have you purposely hyperventilate, which leads to tingling sensations and dizziness much like a panic attack. As the symptoms build, you practice controlled-breathing or relaxation exercises that short-circuit the panic reaction and allow you to stay in control of your fear. Repeated exercises of this sort undercut the fear of fear that can escalate everyday anxiety into full-scale panic.

Some behavioral psychotherapists take this part of

the treatment a step further, in a technique called flooding, by directly exposing you to situations that have
prompted panic in the past. If public transportation has
been an issue, the psychotherapist and you might go
for a subway ride together. This approach allows the
psychotherapist to teach relaxation techniques on the
spot, right where they count the most. It's something
like learning to speak French by flying to Paris for the
weekend.

Cognitive psychotherapy arose in the late 1960s
when Aaron Beck, M.D., of the University of Pennsylvania developed a new approach to understanding
depression. Beck's cognitive psychotherapy stands Freud
and classical psychoanalysis on their respective heads.
For Freud, emotion hidden under layers of repression
creates behavior. In other words, how we feel determines how we think. No, says Beck, it's the other way
around—how we think determines how we feel. The
key to feeling isn't buried emotion. It's cognition—
that is, what we believe to be true, and how we ac-
quire and process information about ourselves and
our world.

Cognitive psychotherapy looks at the basic premises
we use to interpret and make sense of our environment.
These premises are as automatic as reflexes. They pop
up instantaneously, like the instructions coded into
computer software when you input a command. Cognitive premises are healthy, or adaptive, if they help us get
along in the world. They are maladaptive, or unhealthy,
if they cause us trouble based on false information or
conclusions.

Beck and other experts propose that the anxiety
underlying panic disorder draws on two maladaptive
premises. First, people with panic disorder see the
world as dangerous and overwhelming. It is full of

frightening and terrible things all just waiting to happen. Second, individuals with the disease figure they lack the skills, strength, and ability to cope with such a threatening world. There's simply too much out there for them to ever stand up to it all.

These two key beliefs lead to three more central cognitive errors. The first is *vulnerability*. "I felt panic in this place before," the individual says. "I'm sure to feel it again." Next there's *escalation*. "If I feel even a little anxiety, it's bound to get worse and blow up into a panic attack. I'm safe only when I have no symptoms at all, not even a little one." The final belief is *inability to cope*. "If and when I have an attack, I can't help myself. I need somebody to lean on."

The collision of these mistaken and maladaptive beliefs causes panic disorder, particularly in individuals with a biological predisposition to the disease. The belief in a dangerous world and the patient's sensations combine to produce panic. The panic in turn spawns fear of subsequent attacks and creates the anticipatory anxiety that leads to phobic avoidance.

Beginning in the 1980s, cognitive and behavioral psychotherapies were combined to create what we now know as cognitive-behavioral therapy. The combination makes sense since both approaches emphasize learned responses—the one of physical and psychological reactions, the other of deeply held belief systems.

What happens in cognitive-behavioral psychotherapy?

The cognitive aspect of this therapy begins with teaching you to recognize your automatic cognitive premises for what they are. The next step is to check them out and see if they're true.

In the initial therapy sessions, the psychotherapist

works with you to identify specific fears and the meaning you give to them. For example, you might firmly believe that even a mild elevation of heartbeat can prompt a heart attack. At the same time, the psychotherapist has you describe just how a panic attack feels in terms of symptoms, emotions, and the thoughts running through your mind during the episode. Then the psychotherapist asks you to assess the panic attack in retrospect—"Looking back, how dangerous do you think it was? Were you really about to die?"

Putting this information together allows the psychotherapist to create a summary picture of your typical panic attack. In the process, he or she can begin showing you how a distorted belief—for example, that elevated heartbeat leads to heart attack—plays into the initial anxiety and the panic escalating from it.

Homework is part of the behavioral aspect of cognitive-behavioral psychotherapy. The assignment from the psychotherapist might be to keep a journal on how you react, feel, or think in certain settings. Say you've had trouble with panic attacks on public transportation. Your assignment might be to keep a close record of what you're thinking as you board a bus or subway train. Reading this record back later makes you aware of cognitive distortions, such as the notation, "Doesn't anybody know how often these stupid things derail and everybody on board gets killed?" Later, you may be asked to go back and rewrite such distortions into language that better fits reality: "For all the miles they travel and people they carry, trains really have few accidents."

In addition to homework, a cognitive-behavioral psychotherapist may also incorporate such behavioral techniques as relaxation training or flooding.

Is cognitive-behavioral psychotherapy successful against panic disorder?

Research studies have evaluated the effectiveness of cognitive-behavioral psychotherapy in treating panic disorder since the early 1980s. The data show that this approach does work, and relatively quickly. Most cognitive-behavioral panic disorder programs last about twelve weeks, and 60 to 80 percent of patients respond well within that time. Some are completely symptom-free, while others may still have trouble with panic but are better able to function on a day-to-day basis.

It is unclear, however, how long-lasting the benefits of cognitive-behavioral psychotherapy are. Many patients go through periods where they function well, only to suffer a relapse of symptoms some months or years later. Longer-term psychotherapy may be necessary as a result.

Cognitive-behavioral psychotherapy also appears to work well in combination with medication. The medication treats the disorder by regulating abnormal neurotransmitter function, at the same time that the psychotherapy reverses old conditioning and distorted thinking patterns around fear and helps you learn to respond to the environment in ways other than panic. Such combined therapy appears to work best with highly anxious patients or those who are reluctant to enter psychotherapy.

Does a given psychotherapist use only one form of psychotherapy? Do I have to be concerned about choosing the "right" professional?

Most psychotherapists are trained in a variety of psychotherapeutic disciplines in the course of residency or graduate school. They can use the one that best fits their own theoretical orientation and expertise and that also suits your needs. What works for you may not work as well for other patients, or vice versa.

Psychotherapists can also use a pluralistic approach. That is, they may employ various modalities to come up with an approach that's uniquely suited to you. Certain elements of PFPP, for example, can be woven into a more straightforward cognitive-behavioral method to address issues specific to your situation.

Once I choose a psychotherapist to work with, how will he or she select a psychotherapeutic method?

By and large it will depend on what you need and the choice the psychotherapist feels competent to make. A good psychotherapist is adept at matching a patient's personality style and needs to a psychotherapeutic modality. Here are two patients, each with different styles and needs, and the methods selected by their psychotherapists as best suited to them.

Jon always took a seat at the head of the class. He finished a small liberal arts college in three years, went directly to graduate school, completed his Ph.D. by the time he was 24, and won an assistant professorship at a prestigious university. Not long after he took up his academic position, he experienced a panic attack. Soon the seemingly random episodes escalated into panic disorder.

Jon was referred to a psychiatrist. Only a few minutes into his first psychotherapy session, Jon said, "Let's be clear. I don't hold with this Freudian stuff. I'm not interested in telling you about my childhood. I have a problem I want to fix. Let's figure out what's wrong and solve it."

The psychiatrist quickly recognized Jon as a highly intellectual, data-driven individual oriented to the here-and-now. He decided on a cognitive-behavioral psychotherapeutic program that focused on Jon's mistaken cognitions—a tendency to think that his entire sense of self-worth depended on absolute success in everything, no matter how small—and instructed him in self-relaxation skills to overcome the onset of panic symptoms. This approach worked. Within four months, Jon was practically symptom-free.

Marie's panic attacks began when her boss—a manipulative, self-serving man who put his own career above all else—asked her to take on a great deal more responsibility without any increase in salary. Feeling used but desperately fearful that saying no would cost her the job, Marie agreed. She experienced her first panic attack a few days later. Over the next several months she developed all the symptoms of panic disorder, including an agoraphobia that made commuting practically impossible.

Over the course of her first few meetings with a psychotherapist, Marie spoke of a difficult, demanding childhood. The eldest of several children, Marie was expected to act as a surrogate parent from the time she was only three years old. Neither parent was emotionally available. Her father was an ambitious attorney who worked nights and weekends to become a partner in a major litigation firm. He came home only to sleep and shower. Her mother, a shy, withdrawn woman, felt incompetent as a mother with such a large family and doubted her ability to support her husband's rising career. Inconsistent and emotionally erratic, she pushed many of the duties of mothering onto Marie, who essentially grew up without a true childhood.

The psychotherapist recognized quickly that the young woman's panic arose from conflicts over deeply repressed anger that had originated while Marie was growing up. These conflicts were now being reawakened by events at work. The psychotherapist selected PFPP as the best approach to help Marie activate the old feelings, deal with them directly, and develop new ways of handling anger and asserting herself against exploitative situations. Although this approach took a full year to complete, Marie overcame her panic attacks and agoraphobia. She moved on to a better-paying job under a supervisor she respected.

Do I need to know what approach my psychotherapist is using?

You have every right to know what approach your psychotherapist is following and why he or she thinks it is the best one for you. Understanding what is being done and why can help in your healing.

How often do psychotherapy sessions occur, and how long do they last?

A typical psychotherapy session lasts forty-five to fifty-five minutes. Except for classical psychoanalysis, which often follows a five-days-a-week schedule, most psychotherapists meet with their patients once each week. In the initial period, you might see your psychotherapist twice a week to get the process off to a running start, particularly if you are having great difficulty functioning.

What does a psychotherapy session cost?

It varies with the professional and the region of the country. Psychiatrists on the East and West coasts charge between $100 and $300 per session. Psychologists in the same areas have fees that are usually a little less. Rates also drop in the intermountain West, the Midwest, and the South. Licensed clinical social workers and marriage, family, and child counselors have lower fees than psychologists or psychiatrists.

How long will it take before I feel better?

You may experience a sense of relief almost immediately, simply because you have taken direct action to confront the disease. Typically you can expect to be feeling markedly better within ten to twelve weeks.

The overall length of therapy depends on a number of things, including the severity of your panic disorder, the psychotherapeutic approach, the psychotherapist's skill, and the effects of any antipanic medications you are taking. When you begin psychotherapy, it is reasonable to ask the psychiatrist how long you can expect the whole process to take. Often, after several sessions, your psychotherapist can estimate the likely course and length of the psychotherapy.

Will I enjoy psychotherapy, or am I going to dread it?

You'll probably feel both ways, depending on what's happening with the psychotherapeutic process, your own feelings on a given day, and the relationship with your psychiatrist. Often people experience tremendous insights in psychotherapy as they suddenly understand emotional issues that have long troubled them. Then again, there are those days when facing up to the disease and its implications is more than you want to bear. As with any demanding activity and complex relationship, you can expect the full range of emotions from happy to sad, loving to angry, joyful to grief-filled. In fact, if you always look forward to psychotherapy, or if you always loathe even the idea of going, something is probably very wrong.

My psychiatrist has prescribed medication for my panic disorder. Won't that get in the way of psychotherapy?

Not at all. Some patients worry that alleviating panic symptoms with medication may take away the motivation to engage in psychotherapy. In fact, many psychotherapists believe quite the opposite. They maintain that medication actually makes the process easier because it removes anxiety over panic attacks, restores a higher level of functioning, and gives you the capacity for concentration needed to pursue psychotherapy. With physical symptoms controlled and no longer a constant object of preoccupation, you are better able to stand back, understand what is going on in your life, and take action to fix it.

The psychiatrist I am seeing is very attractive. What happens if sexual feelings arise in me?

The transference between patient and psychotherapist can involve romantic and sexual feelings as well as any other emotions. It happens so commonly that there's a name for it: erotic transference.

If you have the sense that you're developing a crush on your psychotherapist, the best thing to do is to bring it up. Remember: This is a usual and normal part of psychotherapy. Psychotherapists are trained to deal with erotic transference without making you feel ashamed or abnormal. In fact, uncovering and dealing with the cause of your erotic feelings may provide important insights into the psychological dynamics contributing to your panic disorder.

Psychotherapists are prohibited by a strict code of professional ethics against taking personal advantage of erotic transference. Any response, whether verbal or physical, to a statement of affection or desire is out of place. And be aware that sexual contact of any kind between a psychotherapist and his or her patient is never justified. Sexual misconduct is such a serious ethical violation of the professional relationship with the patient that it can cost a psychotherapist his or her license to practice.

I'd like to know my psychotherapist socially, maybe have dinner and take in a movie. Is this okay?

Wanting your psychotherapist as a friend is a natural reaction. In fact, it affects almost everyone who enters psychotherapy. There's nothing wrong with the feelings themselves; they arise naturally from transference.

However, the nature of psychotherapy precludes having your therapist as a good friend. After all, the relationship between the two of you offers a special intimacy and trust unavailable in the usual friendship. Take advantage of the psychotherapeutic relationship for what it is. Don't try to make it into something different—and less useful for you.

I've had certain experiences and feelings in my life that I don't want to share with anyone. Is it okay for me to hold back this kind of thing in psychotherapy?

Yes, you may. Say up front that there is material you want to keep private. Your psychotherapist should be willing to respect the boundary you've drawn.

But be aware that the material you've decided to keep private may hold important information about your panic disorder. If you find that psychotherapy isn't progressing well, it could be that what you're keeping private is holding you back. At this point, be willing to discuss the privacy issue further with your psychotherapist.

Also, don't lie or invent fictions to protect your privacy. Sometimes patients try this, even as a way of testing psychotherapists to see just how smart they are. All lying does is confuse matters. Your psychotherapist isn't a mind reader, and if you want to deceive him or her, you can almost certainly pull it off. It won't do you any good, and it will sidetrack or derail the psychotherapeutic process.

I don't want the details of my life bandied about all over town. How can I be sure that my psychotherapist will keep private matters private?

Confidentiality is a moral cornerstone of psychiatrists, psychologists, social workers, and other psychotherapists. Psychotherapists can lose their licenses over breaches of confidentiality, and any psychotherapist who tells stories about patients to friends and acquaintances will soon find his or her sources of referral drying up. Other professionals won't recommend a psychotherapist who can't respect patients' privacy.

The only time a psychotherapist is legally obligated to breach confidentiality arises with a patient who is imminently suicidal. In such a case the psychotherapist must intervene. He or she has to contact family and friends about the danger and either persuade the patient to agree to hospitalization or contact the local rescue squad to arrange transit to a hospital. There the patient will be safe and can be further evaluated.

Psychotherapists see twenty, thirty, maybe even thirty-five patients a week. How do they keep from confusing one patient with another?

Tracking each patient as an individual is something psychotherapists learn how to do. Psychotherapists in training take pages and pages of notes in each session as a way of learning how to listen and to remember key details. Sometimes they even tape-record sessions with the patient's permission. As psychotherapists advance in skill, they become expert at active listening, concentrating on what's important and remembering it in remarkable detail. Pretty soon it becomes a learned skill that's never forgotten.

Does psychotherapy ever backfire?

Yes, for a number of possible reasons. The psychotherapist may not be skilled, or he or she may have selected the wrong approach for the patient. As an example, in the case of Jon—the fast-track academic—panic-focused psychodynamic psychotherapy would have been a wrong choice. Frustrated by the insistence that he look at conflicts over loss, separation, and anger when he wanted to learn a set of techniques to control his panic reactions, Jon would eventually quit therapy in frustration. He could end up untreated, still plagued by his disease.

Sometimes, too, patients destroy the process themselves, out of open or hidden feelings of self-destructiveness. Deep down, because of low self-esteem or other reasons, they don't want to get better.

Can a support group help in treating panic disorder?

As a substitute for psychotherapy, a support group doesn't work. But it can be a great add-on to your psychotherapy. People with mental diseases commonly believe they are the first and only person ever to suffer this particular malady. It can be of great benefit to hear other people with the same disease relate similar experiences. And sometimes shared insights about the disease process can supply important understandings about yourself.

Your psychotherapist may be able to recommend a support group. The appendix also contains information on organizations that sponsor or provide information about group meetings.

Chapter Six

HOW CAN MEDICATION HELP?

If I have panic disorder, will medication be part of my overall treatment?

Often it will be. Pharmacotherapy—the use of medications in the treatment of mental disease—is one of the most important weapons psychiatrists have to combat panic disorder. These days, psychiatrists can use any of a number of medications that have been shown to be highly effective against the disease.

The decision to use medication is one that should be made by you and your doctor in consultation. A number of factors have to be taken into account, including the severity of your disease, any coexisting psychological conditions like depression, your physical health, and your expectations and goals in treatment.

Your own preferences are important too. Some people are by nature willing to take a medication prescribed by a physician without a second thought. Others are suspicious of pills, perhaps because they prefer more natural ways of treating diseases or because they are highly sensitive to the effects and side effects of medications and find the experience unpleasant. Be sure to bring such issues up to your doctor and discuss them frankly and fully.

Aren't psychiatric medications just drugs? And aren't they dangerous?

The word *drug* has two meanings. The first is the medical one. In medicine, a drug is any compound used to diagnose or treat disease, alleviate pain, control or improve an abnormal condition, or change the structure or function of living tissue. By this definition, aspirin is a drug. The other meaning is the one used more on the street, television, and popular parlance—a substance that alters consciousness, often by blocking out some sensations and heightening others. Alcohol, marijuana, cocaine, angel dust, and heroin are examples of common consciousness-altering drugs, both legal and illegal.

Technically, all the pharmacotherapeutic medications (also called psychotropics) prescribed for the treatment of panic disorder are drugs. Physicians use these compounds to improve an abnormal condition in the brain. But they are most certainly not drugs in the street sense, nor are they medically certified alternatives to the various—and often very dangerous—recreational chemicals.

Psychiatric medications are safe when they are used as intended and carefully monitored by a skilled physician. Harm comes from misuse. That's why medications should be taken only when you are in the care of a physician, preferably a psychiatrist with a good background in psychopharmacology. Training background and experience with medications is one of the questions to bring up in selecting a psychiatrist.

I've heard that many psychotropic medications have strong and unpleasant side effects. Should I be concerned?

A side effect is any consequence of taking a medication other than the one intended. Aspirin has two principal physiological effects in the body. It alleviates pain, and it thins the blood, by lessening its tendency to clot. If you take aspirin for a headache, the blood-thinning consequence is a side effect. If you take aspirin for its blood-thinning, headache relief is a side effect.

Similarly, all psychotropic agents have both intended effects, such as alleviating panic symptoms, and side effects, some of which are of no consequence while others can be troubling. As we go through the classes of anti-panic medications, we will lay out their potential side effect to give you a sense of the upside and the downside of each agent.

Keep several points about side effects in mind. First of all, a positive mental attitude helps. If you begin taking a given medication full of the expectation that it will make you put on weight faster than a doughnut-only diet, you'll probably start packing on the pounds overnight. Maintaining a strong focus on the benefits of the medication will actually help it work for you and at the same time minimize any side effects.

Second, no two people react exactly the same. No matter what your best friend told you about his or her experiences on Prozac, you are a wholly different individual. Have faith in your individuality.

Third, don't be afraid to discuss the effects and side effects of any medication with your psychiatrist. Openness between the two of you is important to the success of the therapy.

And finally, be patient. Many side effects result from

the body's adjustment to the medication. The first time you take up a new sport, sore muscles come as no surprise. Similarly, the body may react to a newly introduced medication in unpleasant or disconcerting ways. Once the body adapts to the presence of the new compound, many of the side effects decrease or disappear, typically within two to six weeks. By that time too you will likely be experiencing the positive benefits of the psychotropic medication.

How long can I expect to be on medication? Once I start taking it, will I have to keep on taking it forever?

The length of pharmacotherapy depends on the course of your disease and your response to the medication and any accompanying psychotherapy. Most panic disorder patients treated with psychotropic agents use them for six to twelve months, then reduce the medication and go off it entirely. Still other people use medications successfully, live for some time symptom-free, then experience a return of panic disorder and go back to using medication. A small number of panic disorder cases need to remain on medication indefinitely, as long as the disease persists.

I don't want my doctor to just scribble out a prescription, toss it in my direction, and leave the exam room. What can I expect in terms of information and support?

You'll get much better attention than an unadorned prescription sent flying in your direction during a hurried office visit. Psychiatrists understand that the patient-physician relationship in which the medication is administered is as important to success as choosing the right antipanic drug and determining the effective dosage.

Early on in the relationship, it is important for the psychiatrist to create an atmosphere of trust between the two of you. Realistic and truthful reassurance is also important. You have a right to expect the physician to give you full information about the medication. He or she should demonstrate a willingness to deal with your concerns and with any unexpected problems you might have. It is important too that the physician give you as much explanation as you need on how the medication works, what benefits it will deliver, and when.

If medication is effective against panic disorder, why go to the trouble and the expense of psychotherapy?

There is no magic pill against panic disorder. It's not like a bad headache—two aspirin and a good night's sleep will do wonders. The disease is complex and multifaceted, and it usually requires treatment on more than one front. Medication is useful, but by itself it's usually not enough.

Psychotherapy may shorten the time you need to stay on medication. And a recent study shows that psychotherapy is particularly useful during the transition period, when patients come off medications and adjust to living without them.

More and more psychiatrists hold the opinion that it is irresponsible to prescribe medication for panic attack without some form of psychotherapy. This need not be classical psychoanalysis, and it doesn't have to continue for years and years. At a minimum, though, you should receive brief psychodynamic therapy or supportive psychotherapy along with medication.

Is psychotherapy combined with medication more successful against panic disorder than either one alone?

Probably. Unfortunately, only a few studies have looked at a combination of the two therapies and compared the outcome with the results of doing just one or the other. There is, for example, some evidence that using antidepressant medications along with cognitive-behavioral therapy works somewhat better over the short term. The long-term effect remains up in the air, however. Antianxiety medications are thought to benefit highly anxious patients who are reluctant to enter psychotherapy by helping them to relax enough to profit from treatment.

However, the rigorous data needed to determine the benefits of psychotherapy alone or psychotropics alone versus the two in combination are still lacking. Only when this research is completed sometime in the future will we know for sure what works best.

Most clinicians working on panic disorder do in fact combine psychotherapy with pharmacotherapy. This is particularly true for severe cases of the disease and for patients who show no improvement at all after four to six weeks of psychotherapy alone.

It makes sense that this would be the case. Psychotropic agents block the physiological causes of panic attack, preventing or greatly limiting the effects of unexpected panic attacks. With the medication eliminating the disturbing events that lead to phobic avoidance and anticipatory anxiety, you can return to the places you have learned to avoid without fear that an attack will befall you. The confidence this new freedom creates, particularly when it is put to work in an effective psychotherapeutic program, allows you to face situations that have been troubling and take control of them again—without suffering a panic attack.

Choosing the combination of medication and psycho-therapy right for you entails as much art as science. As a psychiatrist comes to understand the dynamics behind your disease, he or she can determine the medication and psychotherapeutic approach most likely to help you.

How do the panic disorder medications work?

You will remember from chapter 3 that a faulty nerve cell complex, particularly within the brain areas involved in panic, is thought to be a cause of panic disorder. The medications used against panic all work their effects at the level of the nerve cell complex. The exact chemical mechanisms behind their effectiveness against panic attack are unknown, but we do have some idea about how they work at the level of the nerve cell.

The antidepressant drugs used against panic disorder alter the quantity and quality of neurotransmitters involved in panic reactions. For example, imipramine (Tofranil) affects norepinephrine, and fluoxetine (Prozac) works on serotonin. Most likely, these drugs help panic areas of the brain work more efficiently, and they return them to a correct synchrony through their effect on norepinephrine and serotonin. They may also do what is called down-regulation of the adrenergic system, including the locus ceruleus—essentially, reducing the overreaction of neurons in the panic-producing areas of the brain and bringing them back within a normal range.

The antianxiety drugs used against panic disorder, such as clonazepam (Klonopin) and alprazolam (Xanax), increase the release of GABA, a neurotransmitter with an inhibitory or quieting effect on the brain's panic-producing regions. These medications also attach to the benzodiazepine receptors on certain neurons and increase their affinity for GABA. It may also be important that these medications reduce anxiety overall, preventing small worries from growing into big panics.

Which medications have been used successfully against panic disorder?

Four types of psychotropics have demonstrated clear effectiveness against panic disorder:

- tricyclic antidepressants (TCAs)
- monoamine oxidase inhibitors (MAOIs)
- selective serotonin reuptake inhibitors (SSRIs)
- antianxiety medications, or anxiolytics

The table at the end of this chapter lists most of the medications that have been tried against panic disorder and rates their effectiveness. In the table, as in this chapter, the generic name of the compound comes first, followed by the brand name in parentheses.

What are tricyclic antidepressants, and how do they work?

These medications derive their name from their three-ringed chemical structure and their effectiveness in treating depression. The medication that inaugurated the psychotropic treatment of panic disorder in the 1960s was the TCA called imipramine (Tofranil). Originally used against depression, imipramine has also been shown in over a dozen carefully designed studies to stop panic effectively. It is still widely used as a primary antipanic medication.

As with all the other antidepressants, imipramine may in part work against panic disorder because it also affects depression. The two mental diseases often go hand in hand. Up to 80 percent of patients with panic disorder suffer from major depression as well.

When imipramine is given specifically against panic, the dosage is often lower than when it is prescribed for depression. Usually the dosage is started at 10 milligrams per day for three days, then increased by 10 milligrams daily until an effective dose is reached. Usually a patient has to take the medication for three to six weeks before the antipanic effect takes hold. Most people with panic disorder react strongly to imipramine and the other tricyclic antidepressants and need relatively low doses, somewhere in the 50 to 200 milligram range. Still, some patients require 300 milligrams or more a day to block panic attacks. Various dosages are needed because different people metabolize imipramine differently, affecting the amount of medication actually circulating in the blood.

Imipramine affects the brain at the neurotransmitter level. After a neurotransmitter has moved from one nerve cell to the next, it is reabsorbed so that a large quantity of this neurotransmitter doesn't build up. For example, if a large amount of norepinephrine accumulates, the receiving nerve cell remains permanently excited. Reabsorption of the neurotransmitter prevents this.

Imipramine works by slowing the rate of reabsorption for the neurotransmitters norepinephrine and serotonin. As a result, larger quantities of these two neurotransmitters are available, establishing correct communication among nerve cells and resulting in down-regulation of the panic-producing areas of the brain. However, despite considerable research into the medication, the complete mechanism of imipramine's antipanic effect remains unclear.

Another tricyclic antidepressant, clomipramine (Anafranil), introduced into the United States only recently, blocks the reabsorption of serotonin. Rigorous comparative studies of this medication show that it is at least as effective as imipramine. Some of the data indicate that it may even be better at blocking panic symptoms. Like imipramine, clomipramine is started at a low dosage and increased until an effective dose is determined.

Two other TCAs, desipramine (Norpramin, Pertofrane) and nortriptyline (Aventyl, Pamelor), are well studied and have been shown to be effective against panic disorder. Amitriptyline (Elavil, Endep), doxepin (Adapin, Sinequan), protriptyline (Vivactil), and trimipramine (Surmontil) have not been studied as carefully as imipramine and clomipramine. However, they too appear to be effective at stopping panic attacks.

What are the advantages and the disadvantages of the tricyclic antidepressants in treating panic disorder?

The TCAs, particularly imipramine and clomipramine, are effective antipanic medications. Simply, they work. Twelve-week trials of tricyclic antidepressants show response rates of 60 to 80 percent. The medication keeps working too. There is no evidence that the body builds up any tolerance to imipramine and needs continuously larger doses. One large study showed that patients continued to respond well to imipramine over an eight-month period.

Imipramine has the added advantage of a long clinical history. Psychiatrists have been using this medication for over thirty years, and they have a considerable body of experience with it. This comfort and expertise with the medication contribute to its effectiveness.

Side effects may be the greatest drawback to the tricyclic antidepressants. Some individuals don't tolerate these medications well, possibly leading them to discontinue pharmacotherapy. This is particularly a problem with panic disorder, since people with the disease are notoriously sensitive to TCAs.

Tricyclic antidepressants often dry out the mouth and cause constipation, blur vision, and cause urinary difficulties and sexual dysfunction. Weight gain can also be a problem. In some individuals these medications affect the heart adversely, requiring further caution among people with cardiac disease. Tricyclic antidepressants are also very dangerous in overdose. They interact with alcohol, and anyone using TCAs must reduce or eliminate drinking. If started on tricyclic antidepressants in overly large doses, a few individuals have an exactly opposite psychological response, becoming excited and nervous rather than calm and relaxed. Seizures occur in a few cases as well, but no more commonly than with other antidepressants. In a percentage of patients, too, tricyclic antidepressants cause postural hypotension—that is, when you stand up from a prone or seated position, blood pressure drops suddenly and you may faint.

Many of these side-effects can be alleviated by carefully determining the lowest effective dose of the medication and taking no more than the minimum needed to stop panic. Sucking sugar-free hard candies helps alleviate dry mouth, and increasing fiber in the diet and drinking more water can overcome the constipation.

Relapse after withdrawal of the medication is also an issue as with any anti-panic medication. Depending on which definition of relapse is used, symptoms return in 30 to 74 percent of patients on imipramine. Turn those numbers around, however, and they mean that between 26 and 70 percent of people who use TCAs suffer no recurrence of panic symptoms after withdrawing from the medication. In some unknown manner, the medication "cures" the illness.

What are monoamine oxidase inhibitors (MAOIs), and how do they work?

As a rule, MAOIs are used in patients who don't tolerate or respond to tricyclic or other antidepressants and need a different psychotropic. Like the tricyclic antidepressants, the monoamine oxidase inhibitors (MAOIs) are highly effective against panic. Also like the tricyclic antidepressants, they work their effect at the level of the nerve cell complex. Outside the neuron, an enzyme known as monoamine oxidase (MAO) prevents the buildup of norepinephrine and serotonin by breaking them down chemically. MAOIs slow the action of this enzyme, thereby permitting an accumulation of neurotransmitters at the receiving nerve cell. Exactly why and how this action blocks panic remains unknown, however.

MAOIs are started at low doses and slowly raised until an effective dosage is found. For example, phenelzine (Nardil) is usually begun at 15 milligrams a day and normally takes effect with a relatively low dose. Similarly, tranylcypromine (Parnate) is initiated at 10 milligrams daily. Still, some people need as much as 75 to 90 milligrams daily of phenelzine to obtain the medication's antipanic effect. Usually three to six weeks on MAOIs are required before panic attacks cease.

What are the advantages and disadvantages of MAOIs in treating panic disorder?

Like TCAs, MAOIs have been around for a long while, and psychiatrists by and large feel comfortable with them. And they are effective, achieving the same 60 to 80 percent response rate as the tricyclic antidepressants. Since MAOIs are antidepressants, they also help resolve any depression accompanying the disease, and they can be used to treat people with both disorders. MAOIs are also much less dangerous in overdose than TCAs. They do not affect the heart adversely, allowing individuals with cardiac disease to take them.

On the downside, MAOIs can have a number of annoying side effects. These include changes in sexual response, weight gain, and postural hypotension. Depending on how relapse is defined, various studies have found the relapse rate with phenelzine to lie between 14 and 100 percent—somewhere between one in seven and seven in seven.

However, the greatest disadvantage to MAOIs is the risk of an extreme hypertensive crisis—an abrupt, dramatic increase in blood pressure—through what is called the tyramine effect. Tyramine, an amino acid, acts as a pressor, a compound that raises blood pressure. Usually, tyramine is kept at normal levels in the bloodstream by the action of monoamine oxidase in the gut. The MAOIs block this protective action, and tyramine may enter the circulatory system in excess. The result can be an episode of dangerously high blood pressure that may lead to a stroke.

If your psychiatrist prescribes MAOIs, you will need to follow a diet that excludes tyramine-rich foods, like aged meats (such as air-cured salami), ripened cheeses (for example, Brie, Camembert, and Roquefort), and wine. You also need to avoid common medications that can raise blood pressure, such as the pseudoephedrine hydrochloride used in many over-the-counter cold remedies and decongestants, diet pills, and local anesthetics combined with adrenaline. For safety, patients on MAOIs carry an antidote medication, such as chlorpromazine (Thorazine), to take in case blood pressure suddenly increases.

What are the selective serotonin reuptake inhibitors, and how do they work against panic disorder?

It was a selective serotonin reuptake inhibitor (SSRI) that revolutionized—or at least drew public attention to—the treatment of major depression. Prozac, the brand name for the SSRI fluoxetine, won considerable acclaim as an effective way to alleviate depression, the most common mental disorder and one of the most disabling.

In 1996 the Federal Food and Drug Administration approved the use of paroxetine (Paxil) for panic disorder. Although the other SSRIs, including fluoxetine (Prozac), have not been officially sanctioned like paroxetine (Paxil), they appear to be equally effective. Many psychiatrists have begun prescribing them against panic.

As you might well expect from their name, the SSRIs work by slowing the absorption of serotonin by the receiving nerve cell. As a result, the neurotransmitter accumulates to a higher-than-normal concentration at the receptor. As with both the tricyclic antidepressants and the MAOIs, it is unknown why this action at the level of the nerve cell complex stops panic—but it does, apparently through some common mechanism that down-regulates, or "quiets," an overactive region in the central nervous system. Although more rigorous research comparing different medications still needs to be done, SSRIs appear to be as effective as tricyclic antidepressants in stopping panic.

Like the other antipanic medications, SSRIs are started at low doses—2.5 milligrams daily for fluoxetine—and increased slowly until the effective dosage is determined. Individuals vary considerably in how much medication they need. For fluoxetine (Prozac) and paroxetine (Paxil), the effective daily dosage can lie anywhere between 5 and 60 milligrams; for sertraline (Zoloft), between 25 and 200 milligrams; for fluvoxamine (Luvox), between 50 and 300 milligrams.

What are the advantages and disadvantages of the SSRIs in treating panic disorder?

SSRIs are as effective, but no more so, than the tricyclic antidepressants and the MAOIs. The greatest advantage the SSRIs offer over the other two classes of antidepressants is their greater safety and more benign side effects. SSRIs don't dry out the mouth or cause constipation as the tricyclic antidepressants do. They do not affect the heart adversely or pose the risk of a hypertension crisis. They are safe in overdose.

SSRIs also offer the advantage of being highly effective against depression. Since depression and panic disorder often go hand in hand, it is clearly beneficial to have the same medication working against both diseases.

Still, SSRIs aren't free of side effects. They make some people feel anxious or sedated. Stomach upset, sleeplessness, headache, and a disturbed sex life are also common side effects. In many cases, the side effects lessen after the body adjusts to the medication, within four to six weeks. Fatigue and sexual dysfunction, however, may increase over time.

What are the benzodiazepines, and how do they work against panic disorder?

The benzodiazepines are a class of medications that have been used for over forty years to treat anxiety. Originally, psychiatrists and pharmacological researchers thought that the benzodiazepines were effective in alleviating the anticipatory anxiety that is part of panic disorder, but not in stopping actual panic attacks. The arrival of high-potency benzodiazepines, such as alprazolam (Xanax) and clonazepam (Klonopin), has changed that thinking, since they have been shown to be effective against panic as well as anxiety. Recent studies show that the conventional benzodiazepines like diazepam (Valium) and lorazepam (Ativan) also work against panic, often in higher doses. As a result, the high-potency medications are the benzodiazepines of choice for the treatment of panic disorder.

Just like the other antipanic medications, benzodiazepines vary in how much is needed to help a given individual. Two to 6 milligrams a day in divided doses is the effective range for alprazolam, and 1 to 4 milligrams for clonazepam. Like the other medications, the course of treatment is usually six to twelve months.

Benzodiazepines apparently work by attaching to the benzodiazepine receptors in the brain that are components of the important and common GABA-benzodiazepine complexes. By activating the benzodiazepine receptor, the medication increases the affinity of the GABA-benzodiazepine complex for GABA. GABA is a generally inhibitory neurotransmitter that slows nerve action. Most likely this effect calms the panic-producing regions of the brain by preventing the overfiring of neurons. However, the exact mechanism of panic prevention remains unknown.

What are the advantages and the disadvantages of high-potency benzodiazepines in treating panic disorder?

The high-potency benzodiazepines are effective medications, both for stopping panic attacks and for alleviating the anticipatory anxiety that is a central part of the disease. Some psychiatrists are of the opinion that the anxiety reduction is particularly important because it better allows you to enter previously stressful situations, such as crossing a bridge, passing through a tunnel, or using public transportation, without fear of panic attack. To take advantage of this effect, psychiatrists commonly combine high-potency benzodiazepines with cognitive-behavioral or another form of psychotherapy to help you learn how to deal with the world in some way besides panic.

The high-potency benzodiazepines have an advantage over the other three classes of antidepressant medications in that they work fast. TCAs, MAOIs, and SSRIs all usually take three to six weeks before the antipanic effect kicks in. Benzodiazepines can put a stop to panic attacks within the first week. That makes them very useful if you or your psychiatrist want symptoms to be alleviated quickly.

One drawback to the benzodiazepines is that they may make you feel sedated—heavy-brained, slow-moving, forgetful, and generally dull. Usually, however, this effect wears off in three or four days as the body adjusts to the medication. Benzodiazepines sometimes cause a decrease in, or loss of, libido.

Many of the unpleasant side effects of the SSRIs, MAOIs, and TCAs do not affect people on benzodiazepines. They produce no dry mouth, constipation, weight gain, cardiac problems, unwanted stimulation, or hypomania (a euphoric state that is the opposite of depression and is characterized by bad judgment and nervousness). Benzodiazepines don't conflict with most other medications, and they are relatively safe in case of an overdose. They do interact with alcohol, like the tricyclic and other antidepressants, and drinking has to be restricted or eliminated.

Benzodiazepines are no better at preventing relapse than the other antipanic medications. According to research studies, half or more of patients treated with benzodiazepines experience a return of symptoms after treatment ends.

Benzodiazepines may also cause addiction. Alprazolam (Xanax) is particularly addictive. Unlike SSRIs, MAOIs, and TCAs, benzodiazepines have a potential for abuse by patients who take them to get "high." Individuals who have a history of alcohol or substance abuse or who is in recovery should rarely take benzodiazepines.

Benzodiazepines tend to flatten mood over time, eliminating both highs and lows. Further, withdrawal from Benzodiazepine needs to be done slowly, since the drug is potentially addictive once it has been taken for several weeks. Tapering too fast can produce severe discomfort, including anxiety, headache, muscle tremors and aches, and insomnia. Withdrawal is most likely to present a significant problem if you:

- have been in treatment for six months or longer
- are over 60 years of age
- have a dependent personality
- are using other medications
- have been taking a short-acting benzodiazepine, such

as alprazolam (Xanax), lorazepam (Ativan), or oxazepam (Serax)

- have experienced withdrawal problems with other medications
- have been taking an unusually large dose of the benzodiazepine
- lack strong family or social support

Are there any medications that have been used against panic disorder and found to be largely ineffective?

Yes, a number of pharmacotherapeutic agents have been tried and discovered to come up short. Some of them include:

Antidepressants. Bupropion (Wellbutrin), a novel or heterocyclic antidepressant, appears to be ineffective against panic disorder. Other compounds in that class, however, may be effective, such as nefazodone (Serzone), and venlafaxine (Effexor). Results with trazodone (Desyrel) are inconsistent. Mirtazapine (Remeron) has not been tested. The tetracyclic antidepressants, amoxapine (Asendin) and maprotiline (Ludiomil), have mixed reports of effectiveness.

Other Antianxiety medications. Buspirone (BuSpar), a common chronic-anxiety medication, and hydroxyzine (Atarax, Vistaril), an antihistaminelike tranquilizer, work poorly if at all against panic. Barbiturates (for example, phenobarbital) and the older sedative hypnotics should be avoided. Patients develop tolerance quickly, and these medications are very dangerous in overdose.

Beta-blockers. These cardiac medicines can stop the heart palpitations that often accompany panic attacks, and they help control somatic symptoms of anxiety, such as tremors and rapid breathing. As a result, they are used to treat anticipatory anxiety, such as stage fright. They do nothing to stop the other symptoms of panic attack, however, or to deal with the biological causes of panic disorder.

How will my psychiatrist choose a medication for me?

He or she will look carefully at the pattern of your disease, the results of the physical exam and any laboratory work, and your medical history in order to choose the type of medication likely to be both most effective and best tolerated. If you are suffering from depression as well as panic disorder, one of the antidepressants makes good sense. If you are free of depression but deeply plagued by agoraphobia, a high-potency benzodiazepine will give you the quickest relief from panic attacks and allow you to start functioning again.

Feel free to discuss with your physician the choice of medication. Decisions made in consultation with your doctor are the ones most likely to work for you.

Psychopharmacological medications are powerful compounds. How can I be sure that it's safe for me to use them?

Psychiatrists are skilled at developing medication treatment plans that suit the medical needs and characteristics of different patients. Before any medication is prescribed, your psychiatrist will order a variety of tests and examinations to assess medication safety. In most cases, this will include a careful medical history, including information about all medications and drugs you have used; a complete blood workup; a physical examination; and an electrocardiogram (EKG). While you are on the medication, you will meet with your psychiatrist in person or over the phone to manage side effects. Regular blood pressure monitoring is important, particularly if you are taking an MAOI or a TCA. Twenty-four-hour coverage by your psychiatrist is critical in case severe problems develop on evenings or weekends.

Be sure to bring up any safety concerns with your psychiatrist. And remember too to be honest about your medical history, including your use or abuse of medications, drugs, and alcohol.

I always worry about what I put into my body. If I don't want to use medication, should I say so—or let the psychiatrist decide?

Tell your psychiatrist your concerns. Psychotropic medication isn't magic. It offers the best chance of success if both physician and patient feel confident about using it in the course of treating your panic disorder. That means you need to be part of the decision. The psychiatrist should listen to your concerns and do his or her best to address them. It could be that the two of you together decide to avoid medication altogether and concentrate on psychotherapy. Or you could go ahead with the medication, choosing a particular agent that is most likely to give you the greatest benefit with fewest side effects.

Take the initiative to act in your own behalf as a smart, informed consumer. Find out all you can about psychotropics; for example, check out the reference sources in the appendix of this book. And if you have any doubts about the best course of action, don't be afraid to consult another psychiatrist for a second opinion.

Above all, it is important to remember that *you* are key to decision making, about medication as well as other aspects of your treatment. No one else can do it for you.

ANTIPANIC MEDICINES

This table lists the major medications used in the treatment of panic disorder and rates their effectiveness. The generic name of the drug comes first, followed by the brand name or names in parentheses.

Antidepressants

Tricyclic Antidepressants (TCAs)

amitriptyline (Elavil, Endep)	effective
clomipramine (Anafranil)	effective
desipramine (Norpramin, Pertofrane)	effective
doxepin (Adapin, Sinequan)	probably effective
imipramine (Tofranil)	effective
nortriptyline (Aventyl, Pamelor)	effective
protriptyline (Vivactil)	probably effective
trimipramine (Surmontil)	probably effective

Monoamine Oxidase Inhibitors (MAOIs)

phenelzine (Nardil)	effective
tranylcypromine (Parnate)	effective

Selective Serotonin Reuptake Inhibitors (SSRIs)

fluoxetine (Prozac)	effective
fluvoxamine (Luvox)	untested in U.S., but probably effective
paroxetine (Paxil)	effective
sertraline (Zoloft)	effective

Tetracyclic Antidepressants

amoxapine (Asendin)	mixed reports of effectiveness
maprotiline (Ludiomil)	mixed reports of effectiveness

Novel or Heterocyclic Antidepressants

bupropion (Wellbutrin)	probably ineffective

mirtazapine (Remeron)	untested
nefazodone (Serzone)	probably effective
trazodone (Desyrel)	mixed reports of effectiveness
venlafaxine (Effexor)	untested in U.S., probably effective

Antianxiety Medications

Benzodiazepines

alprazolam (Xanax)	effective
chlordiazepoxide (Librium)	probably effective
clonazepam (Klonopin)	effective
clorazepate (Tranxene)	probably effective
diazepam (Valium)	probably effective
lorazepam (Ativan)	probably effective
oxazepam (Serax)	probably effective

Miscellaneous Antianxiety Medications

buspirone (BuSpar)	probably ineffective
hydroxyzine (Atarax, Vistaril)	probably ineffective

Chapter Seven

WHAT ABOUT COMPLEMENTARY, ADJUNCT, AND PREVENTIVE APPROACHES?

To tell the truth, I distrust standard medicine. Are there any alternative-medical approaches to treating panic disorder?

There are two parts to this answer. The first has to do with the word *alternative,* which is often attached to therapies that are proposed as equally good substitutes for standard Western medicine. Actually, the word sets up an inaccurate either-or comparison. Other modalities can complement or add to the usual medical norm of medication and psychotherapy, but they don't simply take their place. Instead they go along with them—which makes the words *complementary* or *adjunct* better descriptions of these therapies.

In the specific case of panic disorder, no specific approach has yet been shown to be an effective alternative to psychotropic medication, psychotherapy, or a combination of the two. But there are a number of measures you can take that will help in the treatment of the disease and enhance your care.

I've read about herbs being used in the treatment of psychiatric disorders. Wouldn't herbs be better for me than the synthetic medicines my psychiatrist has prescribed?

A false mystique has been developing around plant medicines over the past twenty years or so. Many people have come to believe that something out of the ground must be better for you than something out of a pill bottle. It isn't that easy, though.

Many of the medications physicians prescribe either come from plants or are synthetic replications of plant compounds. Aspirin was first isolated from willow bark; digitalis, a common heart medication, from the purple foxglove (*Digitalis purpurea*); coumarin, a blood thinner, from tonka beans and sweet clover; and morphine, a powerful painkiller, from the opium poppy. The line between herbal and pharmaceutical medications is at best fuzzy.

Some herbs certainly do have medicinal effects, but others are ineffective. The fact that a medicine originates in plant material does not mean that it works as claimed.

It also doesn't make it unequivocally safe. This world is full of poisonous plants, from rhododendrons and oleanders to deadly nightshade—some of which have, at times, been mistakenly promoted as natural, organic alternatives to prescription medicines.

Herbal medicines are really no different from any other form of medication. And a plant medication that has an effect on the human body is a drug—that is, a substance that changes the structure or function of living tissue. You need to know what you're taking, and to take only what will work. Good information and well-supported studies of results should guide the choices of all medications, whether herbal or pharmaceutical.

Still, something that comes from nature seems more trustworthy to me than a medication from a pharmaceutical company. Isn't that true?

Not at all. Since herbal medicines are not regulated by the Federal Food and Drug Administration as prescription medications are, there is no official standard and no required quality control. When you pick up an herbal preparation, you can't always be sure what you're getting. There's no standardization of purity or dose, for example; one capsule of one preparation might equal three of another. And sometimes medicines are adulterated with herbs other than the ones on the label. Likewise, one herb may be combined with others without any study of possible interactions among the ingredients.

Are any herbal medications effective against panic disorder?

The popular press has mentioned three herbs in relation to panic disorder. As of this writing, however, none has yet been studied carefully enough to demonstrate its effectiveness against the disease.

St. John's wort. This herbal medicine may have some effect on panic disorder, but as yet this is only a supposition without scientific backup. Not a skin growth but a plant—the word *wort* comes from the Old English term for "herb"—St. John's wort (*Hypericum perforatum*) has been used for centuries in Europe as a mild tranquilizer to treat depression and insomnia as well as infectious diseases like colds, influenza, and tuberculosis. Extracts of St. John's wort remain popular herbal medicines in Europe, particularly Germany. St. John's wort is being promoted currently as an antiviral agent against HIV, the cause of AIDS.

Hypericin, a compound found in St. John's wort, is assumed to be the active ingredient. Recently, two careful research studies analyzed the scientific literature on the use of hypericin as an antidepressant. The results indicate that the compound was indeed more effective against mild to moderate depression than a placebo. In general, adverse reactions and side effects were minimal.

Hypericin's effectiveness against depression is interesting because of the positive effect some antidepressants have on panic attacks. To date, however, no rigorous, controlled double-blind studies have been undertaken of hypericin or St. John's wort in the treatment of panic disorder. The herb may work, but then again it may not. Given what we now know, there's no reason to recommend its use against panic disorder.

Taking St. John's wort is not risk-free, either. Cattle that have grazed on large quantities of the herb have been killed because it causes the skin to inflame upon exposure to sunlight. No deaths in humans have been reported, but clearly St. John's wort should be handled with respect.

There is also concern in the medical community about interaction between St. John's wort and the SSRIs. Possible blood pressure increases in patients on tricyclic antidepressants or monoamine oxidase inhibitors are also an issue. If you are taking any of these medications, don't use St. John's wort.

Kava kava. When Captain Cook first sailed into the South Pacific in the late eighteenth century, he found the

Polynesian islanders downing an intoxicating drink they called kava kava. Made from the underground stem of the pepper *Piper methysticum*, kava kava has been taken for centuries throughout the Polynesian and Indonesian islands where the plant grows.

Used as a relaxant and painkiller, kava kava appears to work like a benzodiazepine antianxiety medication, perhaps attaching to the benzodiazepine receptors and increasing the production of GABA. Herbal-remedy enthusiasts promote kava kava as an antidote to the stresses of modern living and a way of alleviating anxiety, restlessness, and insomnia.

No body of careful scientific study of kava kava has been undertaken. If indeed it acts like a benzodiazepine, it could serve as a substitute medication. But without good data on its efficacy, kava kava cannot be recommended.

In fact, until much more is known about it, kava kava should be avoided because it poses a withdrawal risk. If the herb is used daily over an extended period of time and then stopped abruptly, you will experience symptoms that can range in severity from muscle pain, jittery nerves, and headache to a fatal seizure. That is reason enough to avoid kava kava.

Valerian root. This ill-smelling plant (*Valeriana officinalis*), a common and conspicuous native of Europe and north Asia, has been used medicinally since ancient times. The Greek physician and writer Galen (A.D. 129–199) praised its therapeutic qualities—and gave it a derogatory name based on its nose-curling stink. In medieval Europe, valerian root was highly valued and taken against so many maladies—from epilepsy to cholera—that it was sometimes called "all-heal," a name still used in England today.

Valerian root appears to act as a sedative or hypnotic, which calms the central nervous system. Although the herb has been studied as a sleep inducer, it has yet to be researched in the treatment of panic disorder. Currently, though, there's no scientific reason to believe that it helps against panic disorder, and it cannot be recommended.

If I decide I want to try herbs anyway, should I talk to my psychotherapist or internist beforehand?

Absolutely—particularly if you are already on psychotropic medication. Do not, under any circumstances, start taking herbs without checking with your physician or psychiatrist first.

Make no mistake about the possible danger here. An interaction or combined effect between the herb and the medication can seriously threaten your health or life.

Various amino acids have been promoted as medications against a variety of diseases, including mental disorders. Do any of them work against panic disorder?

Amino acids are the fundamental building blocks of protein molecules, and they are absolutely essential to life. Without the right amino acids in our bodies, life cannot be sustained.

The amino acid that has been promoted most as a psychotropic medication is tyrosine, a component of most proteins. Tyrosine is included in at least one commercial herbal remedy that advertises itself as an antidote to depression and stress. There is, however, no scientific evidence to show that tyrosine is effective against any psychiatric disease, including panic disorder. As of this writing, use of tyrosine as a medication cannot be recommended.

Could food allergies have anything to do with panic disorder?

Theoretically yes, but as yet there are no data to show that they do.

From a medical point of view, an allergy is an inflammatory reaction to some compound or material, which is called an allergen. A bee sting is a classic allergic response. The skin inflames—reddens and swells—in reaction to the venom. An allergy can affect any part of the body, including the brain.

In the 1970s, research revealed a connection between red dye no. 2, then a common food ingredient, and a psychiatric disease in children known as attention-deficit hyperactivity disorder (ADHD). After federal regulators ordered the dye removed from foods, there was a great deal of speculation that other additives and ingredients might cause many common psychiatric conditions. The hypothesis remains interesting, but there has been no further finding connecting a food item with mental illness, including panic disorder.

More and more, we're learning that the way one lives has much to do with managing disease. Are there changes in lifestyle that can help me prevent or control panic attacks?

You can take a number of good-sense measures against panic disorder. If you come from a family with a history of panic disorder, you may be able to keep the disease from developing. And if you already have panic disorder, these same measures can help you avoid or limit panic attacks.

Eat a sensible diet. You are what you eat—and following a well-balanced eating plan lays the foundation for physical and mental health. Keep your fat intake down. Emphasize lean proteins like fish and poultry, low-fat dairy products, plenty of fresh fruits and vegetables, and whole grains. Enjoy sweets in moderation if you like them, but make sure they are only a treat, not a principal source of calories.

A good diet pays psychological as well as physical benefits. People with panic disorder typically suffer from a sense of powerlessness against a dangerous and difficult world. Eating healthy brings a sense of overall well-being, and it provides physical mastery. Instead of feeling like a victim, you gain a sense of control. That is an important step on the road to reversing the psychological underpinnings of panic disorder.

Regular sustained exercise. For years now, we've all been barraged with information about the benefits of periodic workouts, particularly against heart disease. Exercise also pays psychological benefits as well.

In the case of panic disorder, you need to pay attention to the type of exercise you do. Short bursts of high-energy activity, like running wind sprints, sharply raise the carbon dioxide level of the blood, increase the amount of lactic acid in the muscles, and boost the breathing rate precipitously. As we saw in chapter 3, these physical changes can prompt a panic attack. Therefore, people with panic disorder should avoid physical activities that entail repeated intense exertion. If you have panic disorder, don't make plans to go the Olympics as a 100-meter sprinter.

But you could consider the 10,000-meter distance run. The best exercise for people with panic disorder raises the heart and breathing rates and holds them steady for an extended period of time. You can do this in a number of ways: running, walking, jogging, bicycling, circuit training in a weight room, and swimming are all good choices. Performing this kind of exercise consistently over time pays a long list of physical benefits. It lowers resting heart rate and blood pressure, reduces cholesterol, burns stored fat, and tones and strengthens muscle.

Working out regularly brings significant psychological benefits as well. Like eating a good diet, it increases your sense of physical mastery and power—the exact opposite of the fear and powerlessness that underlie panic attacks. And exercise actually changes the chemistry of the brain. A long sustained workout like a steady five-mile run increases the release of chemicals called endorphins in the brain. Endorphins are natural opiates, chemicals closely related to the active ingredients that give opium, morphine, and heroin their "feel good" sensation. The increased release of endorphins in exercise creates the so-called runner's high, a natural euphoric state that increases the sense of well-being.

Long slow-distance exercise may also increase the release of serotonin in the brain, although this effect remains unclear. Any rise in serotonin would calm the neuron complex, helping to down-regulate the panic-producing areas of the brain. Exercise may also boost the production of another neurotransmitter called dopamine, which adds to a pleasurable sense of well-being much like that produced by the endorphins.

Despite the many benefits of exercise, don't launch immediately into a training program suited to an experienced marathon runner. Work with someone who is knowledgeable about exercise to develop a program that gradually raises your workout level. And if you are past age 45 or are overweight, be sure to check with your psychiatrist or personal physician before you begin an exercise program.

Avoid recreational chemicals. Marijuana, hallucinogens, cocaine, speed, uppers, downers, angel dust, and all the rest won't do you a bit of good. In fact, they'll cause you positive harm, even set off panic attacks. Stay away from them.

Drink alcohol moderately, or abstain. Since alcohol abuse often accompanies panic disorder, it is wise not to put yourself at risk. Also, alcohol interacts with many of the psychotropic medications used against panic disorder. Usually, for example, patients are advised to avoid alcohol altogether until the right dose of the medication has been established and their reactions to it are stable. At that point, you can talk to your doctor about whether it is safe for you to drink moderately.

Stay away from caffeine, and be careful with chocolate. Caffeine and chocolate belong to a group of chemicals known as the methylxanthines, which are stimulants. They fire up the body by raising heart rate and metabolism and can induce a nervous or jittery feeling. If you are prone to panic attacks, it is easy to misinterpret the effects of a stimulant and fall into the fear that an attack is beginning—which will almost surely bring on the full range of panic symptoms.

Caffeine also competes with benzodiazepine psychotropics for the benzodiazepine receptors in brain neurons. It usually wins too. As a result, using caffeine while you are taking a benzodiazepine essentially reduces its effectiveness.

If you have panic disorder, it's best to avoid caffeine altogether. That can be harder than you think, just because there's more caffeine around than most people are aware of. It's found not only in coffee and tea but also in many soft drinks (clear as well as dark-colored) and over-the-counter medications, such as headache remedies. Be sure to read ingredient labels.

Chocolate, that comfort food par excellence, is fortunately a much milder stimulant than caffeine. An occasional candy bar won't do you any harm. Don't, however, down a pint of chocolate ice cream or share a bag of Halloween treats with your child. A large amount of chocolate can fire your system up as surely as a pot of strong coffee and prompt a panic attack.

Beware stimulants. Many common and widely used over-the-counter medications contain compounds that, like caffeine, raise the heart rate, respiratory rate, and metabolism. Diet pills and stay-awake aids all contain mild stimulants. So do decongestants, cold remedies, and allergy medications that have pseudoephedrine hydrochloride as an ingredient. The name *pseudoephedrine* means "synthetic ephedrine" or "synthetic adrenaline" in Greek, and the compound has adrenalinelike effects, including a distinct rise in blood pressure. Chlorpheniramine maleate, used in allergy and hay fever medications, can also raise blood pressure with sustained use. Any of these medications may set the stage for panic attack.

So can a visit to the dentist—not only because it may involve fear and anxiety, but also because of the local anesthesia used for many dental procedures. Typically, dentists inject patients with a combination of a painkiller like Novocain with adrenaline. The Novocain stops the pain, while the adrenaline closes down the blood vessels in the injected area and keeps the anesthetic from flowing away in the bloodstream, thus lengthening the period of time that a single injection continues to kill pain. In a person with panic disorder, however, the adrenaline can possibly precipitate an attack.

If you have panic disorder and need dental work, talk with your dentist or have your physician or psychiatrist do so. There are two ways around the problem. The first is to use a local anesthetic without added adrenaline, which has to be injected repeatedly during the procedure to eliminate pain. The second is to use the smallest possible dose of added adrenaline to sustain the anesthesia yet not prompt a panic attack.

Don't smoke. For one thing, tobacco will probably kill you long before panic disorder does. For another, nicotine is a strong stimulant. It boosts heart rate and metabolism, increases blood pressure, and constricts blood vessels, particularly the coronary arteries surrounding the heart. Any or all of these effects can set up the chain of physical events that ends in a panic attack.

Sleep well and long. Starting each day rested and refreshed makes you better able to handle the tensions and fears that can induce panic. Most adults require about eight hours of sleep a night, although some people feel fine on less. It's important that you get as much rest as you need. And it's important that your nighttime rest incorporate enough so-called rapid eye movement (REM) sleep. We dream during REM sleep, and dreaming is critical to feeling rested and psychologically at ease. People who miss REM sleep, even if they spend eight hours a night in bed, become tense and irritable. If they have panic disorder, they are much more likely to suffer an attack.

Go to bed and get up at about the same time

every day. And don't drink alcohol right before bed. It may make you drowsy, but when it wears off and rebounds—which you will experience as a racing heartbeat and overall nervousness—you will wake up and likely have trouble going back to sleep.

If I learn to meditate, will it help me control my panic disorder?

Meditation is an excellent skill for anyone who suffers from panic disorder or extreme anxiety.

Meditation comes in many forms—Zen, Vipassana, Tibetan, Hindu, transcendental, and Christian, to name only a few. Whatever the type or style, all meditation is simply a state of focused concentration combined with heightened relaxation and a passive disregard for what is going on around you. That's meditation's real value for someone with panic disorder: it teaches you how to relax even when the outside world is trying its very best to be upsetting, frightening, or irritating. Meditation reverses the onset of panic attack by lowering heart and breathing rate and calming body and mind.

The one problem meditation can pose for someone with panic disorder is learning how to enter a meditative state. Most forms of meditation are based on watching and controlling breathing, in order to turn this normally unconscious reaction into a conscious activity. In someone with panic disorder, however, the focus on breathing can be so terrifying that a panic attack results.

To learn meditation, don't just buy a book or pick up an audiotape. Instead, work in person with a meditation practitioner who knows about your panic disorder and understands how to teach meditation with a focus other than breathing. Since meditation has become an increasingly important tool in the professional psychotherapy community, it may be that your psychotherapist can train you. If not, he or she can likely recommend a meditation teacher. Alternatively, you can make use of the referral sources detailed in chapter 4.

I see newspaper ads for hypnosis as a way of quitting cigarettes. Would it work against panic disorder?

Despite the strange hype and nightclub hucksterism that sometimes attaches to hypnosis, hypnotherapy is a longstanding and well-studied adjunct to psychotherapy. There is a great deal of experience in using hypnosis for breaking habits and addictions like smoking, controlling fear and phobia, and managing chronic pain. To date, little rigorous scientific study has been made of hypnotherapy in panic disorder. But the clinical experience of psychotherapists who have used it in the treatment of panic attack shows that it is very good for general relaxation.

In our normal day-to-day lives, extreme concentration is usually accompanied by high-energy arousal. Hypnotherapy can help you achieve an unusual psychological state, in which you are both very relaxed and able to concentrate deeply. In this state you are open to the suggestion of new ideas. The hypnotherapist can't say to you, "When you wake up, you will no longer suffer from panic disorder," because you'd never believe it. But you will be open to ideas such as "See, now you can relax. Notice how restful and calm you feel right this minute. You have the capacity to be more at ease than you've thought possible."

A hypnotherapist can also teach you methods of self-hypnosis and self-relaxation that are particularly useful against anticipatory anxiety. If you have a fear of bridges and know that an upcoming automobile trip will be taking you over the Golden Gate, you can use self-hypnosis in advance of the crossing to reduce fear and panic symptoms. Some patients become so good at these techniques that they can eliminate antianxiety medications and still avoid the extreme anxiety that may prompt a panic attack.

I've done everything you outline here, yet I still suffer from panic attacks and need to take medication. Should I try harder? Am I doing something wrong?

It's important to keep in mind that panic disorder isn't your fault. You don't suffer from this disease because you're a bad or lazy person. It results from a genetic predisposition, your psychological makeup (which is in large measure inherited), and your life history. Panic disorder isn't the punishment for some sin or crime you committed. It's a disease.

The contemporary trend toward locating the causes of disease in lifestyle has helped us all better understand the role we play in promoting our own health and well-being. But don't take this idea too far and begin to think that all ill health is your fault or that it would go away if you simply tried harder.

Every physician has faced the disappointing situation where a patient follows a therapeutic regimen carefully, yet remains sick. Take adult-onset diabetes, as an example. In many cases, the disease can be controlled well by managing diet and developing an exercise routine. Yet some patients who are absolutely assiduous about their eating and workouts still have to go on regular medication.

The same holds true for panic disorder. Following all

the measures set down here will lower your risk of panic attack. But no matter how hard you work at it, you may still need additional help, from ongoing psychotropic medication, psychotherapy, or a combination of the two.

Be aware too that an impasse may be a sign that your treatment has somehow gone stale. Try shaking things up. You could consult another psychotherapist for a second opinion, for example. Or talk to your psychotherapist about withdrawing from medication for a while and then returning to it later. Sometimes such a new start helps get treatment back on the right track.

Is there anything else I can do to manage my own panic disorder?

Above all else, treat yourself well. It is very important that dealing with the disease not become onerous, burdensome, or depressing. Take time out to give to yourself.

Read the comics. Laugh. Play softball—not because it's good exercise, but because it's fun to get dirty, scream and yell, and mess around with your friends. If you like R&B music, be sure to catch Aretha Franklin or Gladys Knight the next time either one comes to town. Should poetry be your passion, spend the evening with Mary Oliver or T. S. Eliot. Forget staying at the office an hour later tonight. Take your little one to the park and fly a kite. Watch Laurel and Hardy or Mel Brooks on video. Ask your spouse or partner for a massage.

Above all else, let yourself be nurtured. Feeling good does you good; laughter, happiness, and well-being pay psychological dividends. And they help reverse the course of panic disorder. Psychotherapy research has shown that people with panic disorder have great difficulty with separation and independence. Taking care of yourself reminds you that you have value on your own, that you are worthwhile.

Enjoy this life. It's yours. You have every right to all of it, without fear.

Glossary

Words that appear in *italics* are defined within this glossary. Medications are given with the generic name first, followed by the brand name(s) in parentheses.

adrenaline: a hormone produced by the adrenal gland and other organs; increases overall metabolism and readies the body for action, often against a perceived threat; also known as *epinephrine.*

adrenergic system: the various cells, tissues, and organs that either secrete *adrenaline* or are activated by it.

agoraphobia: (Greek, "fear of the marketplace") an extreme and highly developed fear of public spaces, often including stores, auditoriums, churches, buses, trains, bridges, and airplanes.

alprazolam (Xanax): a *benzodiazepine* antianxiety medication effective against panic attack; since this compound is highly addictive, it poses a withdrawal risk.

amitriptyline (Elavil, Endep): a *tricyclic antidepressant* effective in the treatment of panic disorder.

amoxapine (Asendin): a *tetracyclic antidepressant* medication that has been used in the treatment of panic disorder with mixed reports of effectiveness.

anticipatory anxiety: a profound fear or dread of situations an individual thinks likely to prompt a panic attack.

antidepressant: any medication used in the treatment of depression; examples are the *tricyclic antidepressants* and the *selective serotonin reuptake inhibitors.*

anxiety disorders: a group of psychiatric diseases marked by an extremely heightened state of fear; they include *obsessive-compulsive disorder, specific phobia, social phobia, posttraumatic stress disorder,* and generalized anxiety disorder, as well as panic disorder.

anxiolytic: (Greek meaning "anxiety remover") any medication that reduces fear and anxiety; some anxiolytics, such as the *benzodiazepines,* are used to treat panic disorder.

asthma: (Greek, meaning "panting") a condition marked by repeated sudden attacks in which breathing becomes very difficult because of contraction of the bronchial tubes leading into the lungs.

attention-deficit hyperactivity disorder (ADHD): a psychiatric disorder that makes it difficult to focus attention for more than limited periods of time and that is marked by an unusually heightened level of physical activity.

autonomic nervous system: the portion of the brain and spinal cord that regulates the heart, the smooth muscle organs like the intestine, and the glands; functions outside voluntary control.

barbiturate: any of several chemical derivatives of barbituric acid used medically as sedatives and hypnotics; since barbiturates are highly addictive and dangerous in overdose, they are not used in the treatment of panic disorder.

behavioral inhibition: a marked aversion and fear of new people, places, and things; considered an inherited personality trait.

behavioral theory of panic disorder: a scientific explanation of panic disorder as a learned response to feared stimuli in the outside environment or within the body itself.

benzodiazepine: a class of antianxiety medications that affect the action of brain neurons by attaching to *benzodiazepine receptors.*

benzodiazepine receptor: a portion of the common *GABA-benzodiazepine* receptor of the neuron; involved in the uptake of the *neurotransmitter* gamma-aminobutyric acid; the site of attachment for *benzodiazepine* medications.

bupropion (Wellbutrin): a heterocyclic antidepressant; probably ineffective in the treatment of panic disorder.

buspirone (BuSpar): a widely used antianxiety medication; probably ineffective against panic disorder.

cardiac arrhythmia: any variation in normal heartbeat.

cardiopulmonary: referring to the heart (cardio-) and lungs (-pulmonary).

chlordiazepoxide (Librium): a *benzodiazepine* antianxiety medication; probably effective against panic disorder.

classical conditioning: a form of learning in which an individual learns to associate two unrelated events, such as a panic attack while crossing a bridge.

classical psychoanalysis: the approach to psychotherapy developed by the Austrian neurologist Sigmund Freud (1856–1939) and based upon the concept that deeply hidden, unconscious feelings direct human behavior and emotion.

clomipramine (Anafranil): a *tricyclic antidepressant* that is effective against panic disorder.

clonazepam (Klonopin): a *benzodiazepine* antianxiety medication; effective against panic disorder.

clorazepate (Tranxene): a *benzodiazepine* antianxiety medication; probably effective against panic disorder.

cognitive-behavioral psychotherapy: an approach to the psychotherapeutic treatment of panic disorder that blends behavioral techniques, such as *flooding,* with exercises that uncover and examine maladaptive beliefs about the world and the self.

cognitive theory of panic disorder: a scientific explanation for panic disorder as the result of distorted thinking; learned, deeply held beliefs that the world is threatening and the individual powerless against it underlie panic.

computed axial tomography: an imaging technology that allows detailed investigation of the structure of the body, including the brain.

depression: a psychiatric syndrome that consists of sad or flat mood, slowed physical movement, lack of pleasure, lack of interest, changes in sleep and appetite, and sometimes suicidal feelings.

desipramine (Norpramin, Pertofrane): a *tricyclic antidepressant* that is effective against panic disorder.

diazepam (Valium): a *benzodiazepine* antianxiety medication that is probably effective against panic disorder.

differential diagnosis: the process by which a physician selects the probable causes of a patient's symptoms and attempts to identify the one most likely to be the source of the distress.

doxepin (Adapin, Sinequan): a *tricyclic antidepressant* that is probably effective against panic disorder.

electrocardiogram (EKG): a medical test that graphically traces the electric current produced when the heart muscle contracts; commonly used in assessing the cardiac health of a patient.

electroencephalogram (EEG): a medical test that records electrical impulses on the scalp as evidence of nerve activity within the brain; commonly used in the *differential diagnosis* of disorders of the central nervous system.

electrolyte: a molecule that can conduct electrical impulses; for example, signals are sent through the body of a *neuron* by the action of electrolytes; examples are sodium and potassium.

endocrine glands: organs that secrete *hormones* to regulate the action of other organs; examples are the adrenals, the thyroid, the ovaries, and the testes.

endocrinologist: a physician who specializes in diagnosing and treating abnormalities of the endocrine glands.

endorphin: a class of naturally occurring compounds in the brain that are closely related to the *opiate* chemicals found in morphine, opium, and heroin; the source of runner's high and other euphoric postexercise states of mind and body.

ephedrine: a compound isolated from the several plant species of the genus *Ephedra;* used medically to widen the bronchial tubes leading into the lungs; both herbal and medical preparations can produce the symptoms of panic attack.

epinephrine: a hormone produced by the adrenal gland and other organs that increases overall metabolism and readies the body for action, often against a perceived threat; also known as *adrenaline.*

erotic transference: a specific variety of *transference,* in which the patient attaches sexual feelings onto a psychotherapist; often represents a way of avoiding the psychotherapy.

flooding: a commonly used technique of behavioral therapy for the treatment of phobias, panic disorder, and anxiety; the patient is presented with the feared stimulus under controlled conditions as a way of learning how to respond without panic and fear.

fluoxetine (Prozac): a well-known *selective serotonin reuptake inhibitor* antidepressant that is effective against panic disorder.

fluvoxamine (Luvox): a *selective serotonin reuptake inhibitor* antidepressant that is effective against panic disorder

GABA-benzodiazepine complex: one of the most common and

widespread receptors on the neuron; involved in the uptake of *gamma-aminobutyric acid (GABA)*, a *neutrotransmitter*.

gamma-aminobutyric acid (GABA): a *neurotransmitter*; generally has the effect of calming or slowing neuron activity.

heterocyclic antidepressant: any of a class of antidepressant medications so named because of their variable chemical structure.

hormone: a chemical substance produced by one organ of the body to regulate the action of another organ.

hydroxyzine (Atarax, Vistaril): an antihistamine type of anti-anxiety medication that is probably ineffective against panic disorder.

hyperglycemia: an abnormally high level of sugar in the bloodstream.

hypericin: the compound thought to be the active ingredient in the medicinal herb *St. John's wort;* has been shown to work against mild to moderate *depression,* but its effectiveness against panic disorder has not been demonstrated.

hypertension: an acute or chronic condition in which blood pressure remains above normal levels; also known as high blood pressure.

hypertensive crisis: a sudden dramatic increase in blood pressure; can result in a stroke.

hypoglycemia: an abnormally low level of sugar in the bloodstream.

imipramine (Tofranil): the first *tricyclic antidepressant* used effectively against panic disorder; still widely prescribed in treatment of the disease.

irritable bowel syndrome: a condition in which the intestine is abnormally sensitive, subject to cramps and persistent diarrhea.

kava kava: an intoxicating drink made from the underground stem of a species of pepper plant (*Piper methysticum*) native to the South Pacific; apparently works like a *benzodiazepine;* repeated use may cause withdrawal symptoms; to date, its effectiveness against panic disorder has not been studied.

licensed clinical social worker (L.C.S.W.): a *psychotherapist* who has trained by doing graduate study in social work and completing an internship in a clinical mental health setting.

locus ceruleus: (Latin, "blue place") a structure in the brain stem that is rich in *epinephrine-* and *norepinephrine-* producing cells; probably involved in panic attacks.

lorazepam (Ativan): a *benzodiazepine* antianxiety medication that is probably effective against panic disorder.

ma huang: (Chinese) a common name for any of several plants that are the source of *ephedrine*.

magnetic resonance imaging (MRI): a visualization technology that allows detailed investigation of the structure of the body, including the brain.

maprotiline (Ludiomil): a *tetracyclic antidepressant* that is probably ineffective against panic disorder.

medulla oblongata: (Latin, meaning "oblong core") a structure in the base of the brain that deals with the rate of respiration, circulation, and other basic functions of the body.

methylxanthine: any of a group of compounds, including caffeine and the active ingredients in chocolate, that act as stimulants in the human body; generally avoided by people with panic disorder.

migraine: a severe, extremely painful headache accompanied by heightened sensitivity to light, nausea, vomiting, and constipation or diarrhea.

mirtazapine (Remeron): a *heterocyclic antidepressant* that is probably effective against panic disorder.

mitral valve prolapse: a condition in which the valve separating the two left-hand chambers of the heart protrudes into the lower chamber; often benign, mitral valve prolapse sometimes produces symptoms similar to those of panic attack.

monoamine oxidase (MAO): an enzyme that controls the concentration of the neurotransmitters *norepinephrine* and *serotonin* by breaking them down chemically.

monoamine oxidase inhibitor (MAOI): any of a class of *antidepressant* medications that appear to work by inhibiting the action of *monoamine oxidase*, thus allowing the concentrations of norepinephrine and serotonin to rise.

nefazodone (Serzone): a heterocyclic antidepressant that is probably effective against panic disorder.

nerve cell complex: the system comprising a *neuron*, or nerve cell, *neurotransmitters*, and *receptors*.

neurologist: a physician who specializes in diseases and disorders of the nervous system.

neuron: nerve cell.

neurotransmitter: any compound that transmits information from one nerve cell to another; the neurotransmitters significant in panic disorder are *norepinephrine, serotonin,* and *gamma-aminobutyric acid.*

noradrenaline: another name for *norepinephrine.*

noradrenergic system: the various cells, tissues, and organs that either secrete *noradrenaline* or are activated by it.

norepinephrine: a hormone secreted by neurons that serves as a *neurotransmitter* in various parts of the nervous system.

nortriptyline (Aventyl, Pamelor): a *tricyclic antidepressant* that is effective against panic disorder.

obsessive-compulsive disorder (OCD): a mental disorder characterized by the persistent intrusion of unwanted, repetitive thoughts that compel the individual to perform rituals like handwashing or checking locks.

operant conditioning: a form of learning in which an individual learns to perform or avoid an action because of its positive or negative outcome.

opiate: a medication, such as morphine, derived from opium; also includes other compounds, such as *endorphins,* that have effects similar to opium-based pharmaceuticals.

otolaryngologist: a medical doctor who specializes in diseases and disorders of the ears (oto-), nose, and throat (laryng-).

oxazepam (Serax): a *benzodiazepine* antianxiety medication that is probably effective against panic disorder.

pancreas: a large gland situated in the abdomen behind the stomach; secretes a number of digestive enzymes and the *hormone* insulin, which regulates blood sugar level.

panic-focused psychodynamic psychotherapy (PFPP): an approach to the psychological treatment of panic disorder that emphasizes current issues of separation and autonomy in the individual's life; draws heavily from Freud and therapy-based research.

paroxetine (Paxil): a *selective serotonin reuptake inhibitor* used as an *antidepressant* that is also effective against panic disorder.

pavor nocturnus: (Latin, "fear in the night") a period of abrupt, heightened anxiety during the hours of darkness; in children, it often causes them to cry out and startle awake.

pharmacotherapy: the use of medications in the treatment of psychiatric disorders.

phenelzine (Nardil): a *monoamine oxidase inhibitor* that is used as an *antidepressant* and is also effective against panic disorder.

phobia: (Greek, meaning "to be frightened") a persistent, abnormal, irrational fear or dread.

phobic avoidance: the development of a fear so strong that the individual steers completely clear of any situation where the object of that fear might arise.

pluralistic psychotherapy: the use of elements from more than one psychotherapeutic approach in the treatment of a given individual.

positron emission tomography (PET): an imaging technology that allows detailed investigation of the activity of cells and tissues, including those of the brain; shows function as well as structure.

post-traumatic stress disorder (PTSD): a psychiatric illness in which an individual relives the emotions of a particularly frightening or horrific event long after the event occurred.

postural hypotension: a sudden drop in blood pressure upon standing up from a sitting or reclining position.

pressor: any compound that raises blood pressure.

protriptyline (Vivactil): a *tricyclic antidepressant* that is probably effective against panic disorder.

pseudoephedrine hydrochloride: a medication used as a nasal decongestant in cold and allergy medications; side effects include increased blood pressure and overall stimulation, including the jitters in some individuals.

psyche: (Greek, meaning "mind") a general term for the mind, both conscious and unconscious; includes judgment, thought, emotion, and memory.

psychiatrist: a medical doctor who specializes in the diseases and disorders of the mind.

psychic: referring to the *psyche*.

psychodynamic psychotherapy: an approach to the psychological treatment of mental disorders that is derived from *classical psychoanalysis* and focuses on key incidents in the individual's emotional development and maturation.

psychological theory of panic disorder: any of a number of approaches to understanding and treating mental disease by focusing on the patients' *psyche;* an example is *classical psychoanalysis*.

psychologist: a mental health practitioner who has completed doctoral work (either a Ph.D. or a Sci.D.) and a clinical internship.

psychopharmacology: the use of medications to treat psychiatric disorders and to manage the mental illnesses of physically sick people.

psychotherapist: any of various professionals who specialize in treating mental disorders; may be a *psychiatrist*, a *psychologist*, a *licensed clinical social worker*, or a state-licensed registered nurse (R.N.).

psychotropic: any medication that can affect mental state.

receptor: the portion of the nerve cell membrane that reacts to *neurotransmitters* released by other nerve cells.

repression: an unconscious mental activity by which unacceptable thoughts and feelings, usually of an aggressive or sexual nature, are hidden away in the unconscious mind; a central idea in the work of Sigmund Freud, the founder of *classical psychoanalysis*.

selective serotonin reuptake inhibitor (SSRI): any of a class of medications used in the treatment of both depression and panic disorder; they work by slowing the absorption of *serotonin*, a *neurotransmitter* that, in some manner, calms or down-regulates the panic-producing areas of the brain.

separation anxiety: an abnormal fear or dread of being deprived of the physical presence of another person, usually an authority figure like a parent.

serotonergic system: the nerve cells that either secrete or are activated by *serotonin*.

serotonin: an important *neurotransmitter*; usually has an antipanic and antidepression effect.

sertraline (Zoloft): a *selective serotonin reuptake inhibitor* that is used as an *antidepressant*; also effective against panic disorder.

single-photon emission computed tomography (SPECT): an imaging technology that allows detailed investigation of the activity of cells and tissues, including those of the brain; shows function as well as structure.

social phobia: an abnormal fear or dread of settings in which one's behavior is seen or judged by groups of people.

sociological theory of panic disorder: an explanation of panic disorder that places the origin of the disease in the social environment, particularly major life passages, such as graduation from school, getting married, or having a child.

somatic: (Greek, meaning "body") pertaining to the body, as contrasted with the *psyche*.

specific phobia: an abnormal fear, dread, or *phobia* of a particular object or situation; spiders, snakes, and airplanes are common.

St. John's wort: a European plant, *Hypericum perforatum*, that has long been used medicinally and has been shown to be effective against mild to moderate depression; no data to date support its use against panic disorder.

supportive psychotherapy: a psychological approach to the treatment of mental disease that emphasizes the teaching of improved coping skills.

synapse: the region where two adjacent nerve cells come into contact.

tachycardia: an excessively rapid heartbeat, usually over 100 per minute.

temporal lobe: a well-defined portion of the brain that lies along each side of the head, behind the eyes and above the ear.

tetracyclic antidepressant: any of a class of medications used to treat depression; named for their four-ringed chemical structure.

tetrahydrocannabinol (THC): the compound that is the active ingredient in marijuana.

therapeutic alliance: the conscious, willful agreement, both explicit and implicit, made between psychotherapist and patient to work together toward the goal of overcoming the patient's psychological difficulties.

tranquilizer: a medication used to calm feelings of fear and anxiety; also known as an *anxiolytic*.

transference: a complex, unconscious, unwilled psychological process in which a patient in psychotherapy who experiences the awakening of repressed emotions puts those emotions on the therapist; for example, dealing with the therapist as if he or she were the patient's mother.

transient ischemic attack: a short-lived cardiovascular episode involving strokelike symptoms, such as blurred vision or blindness or the inability to walk.

tranylcypromine (Parnate): a *monoamine oxidase inhibitor* that is used as an *antidepressant* and is also effective against panic disorder.

trazodone (Desyrel): a *heterocyclic antidepressant* with mixed reports of effectiveness against panic disorder.

tricyclic antidepressant: a class of medications used to treat *depression;* named for their three-ringed chemical structure.

trimipramine (Surmontil): a *tricyclic antidepressant* that is probably effective against panic disorder.

tyramine effect: an increase in blood pressure due to an abnormal increase in the level of the amino acid tyramine in the bloodstream; it can be a side effect of taking a *monoamine oxidase inhibitor* while continuing to consume tyramine-rich foods, like wine and soft ripening cheeses.

urologist: a medical doctor who specializes in diseases and disorders of the kidneys and urinary tract.

valerian root: not a true root, but the underground stem of a European plant, *Valeriana officinalis,* that appears to act as a hypnotic and sleep aid; no data as yet show its effectiveness against panic disorder.

venlafaxine (Effexor): a *heterocyclic antidepressant* that is not yet tested in the United States but is probably effective against panic disorder.

vertigo: an unpleasant, disturbing sensation in which the environment or surroundings seem to spin around and around; a common symptom of panic attack.

Appendix

FOR FURTHER READING

Agras, M.W. *Panic: Facing Fears, Phobias, and Anxiety.* New York: W.H. Freeman, 1985.

Barlow, David H. *Anxiety and Its Disorders.* New York: Guilford, 1988.

Beck, Aaron, M.D. *Anxieties and Phobias.* New York: Basic Books, 1985.

DuPont, Robert L., M.D. *Phobia: A Comprehensive Summary of Modern Treatments.* New York: Brunner Mazel, 1982.

Fyer, Abby, M.D., Salvatore Manuzza, Ph.D., and Jeffrey D. Coplan, M.D. "Panic Disorders and Agoraphobia." In Kaplan, Harold I., M.D., and Benjamin J. Saddock, M.D., eds., *Comprehensive Textbook of Psychiatry,* 6th ed. Baltimore: Williams & Wilkins, 1995.

Goodwin, D.W., M.D. *Anxiety.* New York: Oxford University Press, 1986.

Gorman, Jack M., and Laszlo A. Papp, eds., "Anxiety Disorders." In Allan Tasman and Michelle B. Riba, eds., *Review of Psychiatry,* vol. 11. Washington, DC: American Psychiatric Press, 1992.

Gorman, J.M., M.D., M.R. Leibowitz, M.D., and D.F. Klein, M.D. *Panic Disorders and Agoraphobia.* Kalamazoo, MI: Current Concepts in Medicine, 1984.

Greist, John H., M.D., James W. Jefferson, M.D., and Isaac M. Marks, M.D. *Anxiety and Its Treatment: Help Is Available.* Washington, DC: American Psychiatric Press, 1984.

McNally, Richard J. *Panic Disorder: A Critical Analysis.* New York: Guilford, 1994.

National Phobia Treatment Directory, 2nd ed. Rockville, MD: Phobia Society of America, 1986.

Otto, Michael W., and Mark H. Pollack. "Treatment Strategies for Panic Disorder: A Debate." *Harvard Review of Psychiatry*, vol. 2 (1994), pp. 166–70.

Pasnau, Robert O., M.D. *Diagnosis and Treatment of Anxiety Disorders*. Washington, DC: American Psychiatric Press, 1984.

Sheehan, David, M.D. *The Anxiety Disease and How to Overcome It*. New York: Charles Scribner & Sons, 1984.

Taylor, C. Barr, M.D., and Bruce Arnow, Ph.D. *The Nature and Treatment of Anxiety Disorders*. New York: Free Press, 1988.

Zane, Manuel D., M.D., and Harry Milt. *Your Phobia*. Washington, DC: American Psychiatric Press, 1984.

ELECTRONIC RESOURCES

Every day there's even more information on the Internet. The following Websites offer a great deal in themselves as well as hypertext links to even more useful locations.

Anxiety Disorder Association of America
http://www.adaa.org
> An excellent resource, for both patients and professionals, that includes a state-by-state list of support groups for people with panic disorder.

Anxiety-Panic Internet Resource
http://www.algy.com.anxiety/
> A grassroots project involving thousands of people—patients, families, and professionals—interested in anxiety disorders. Online support groups are available.

Internet Mental Health
http://www.mentalhealth.com
> A free encyclopedia of mental health information relevant to the understanding, diagnosis, and treatment of mental illness.

Panic Disorder
http://panicdisorder.miningco.com/
> Support groups, bulletin boards, even an article in which SSRIs minimize sexual dysfunction in men.

PubMed
http://www.ncbi.nlm.nih.gov/PubMed/
   An exceptional research resource offering access to 9
   million medical journal articles in the National Library
   of Medicine.

GROUPS AND ASSOCIATIONS

These organizations can help with making psychotherapist referrals, locating support groups, and updating you on the
latest issues in panic disorder treatment.

American Academy of Child and Adolescent Psychiatry
3615 Wisconsin Avenue, N.W.
Washington, DC 20016
(202) 966-7300

American Mental Health Fund
2735 Hartland Road, Suite 335
Merrifield, VA 22081

Anxiety Disorders Association of America
11900 Parklawn Drive, #100
Rockville, MD 20852

Freedom From Fear
308 Seaview Avenue
Staten Island, NY 10305
(718) 351-1717

National Alliance for the Mentally Ill
2101 Wilson Boulevard, Suite 302
Arlington, VA 22201
(703) 524-7600

National Association of Private Psychiatric Health Systems
1319 F Street, N.W., Suite 1000
Washington, DC 20004
(202) 393-6700

National Community Mental Health Care Council
12300 Twinbrook Parkway, Suite 320
Rockville, MD 20852
(301) 984-6200

National Institute of Mental Health
Division of Communications
5600 Fishers Lane
Rockville, MD 20857
(301) 443-3673

National Mental Health Association
1021 Prince Street
Alexandria, VA 22314
(703) 684-7722

DISTRICT BRANCHES OF THE AMERICAN
PSYCHIATRIC ASSOCIATION

APA district branches can help you find a psychiatrist who
lives in your area and has experience in dealing with panic
disorder. Contact the branch nearest to your home.

United States

Alabama
    Dee Mooty, Executive Director
    Alabama Psychiatric Society
    P.O. Box 1900
    Montgomery, AL 36102
    (334) 263-6441 or 800-239-6272 (within Alabama only)
    (334) 269-5200 fax
    E-mail: alapsych@aol.com

Alaska
    Stephanie Gisseman, Executive Secretary
    Alaska District Branch
    6836 Cape Lisburne Loop
    Anchorage, AK 99504
    (907) 377-7311 A.M.
    (907) 278-1383 P.M.
    E-mail: gisseman@sprynet.com

Arizona

Jackie Hyde, Executive Director
Arizona Psychiatric Society
4730 East Indian School Road, #120–101
Phoenix, AZ 85018
(602) 808-9558
(602) 840-5651 fax
World Wide Web: http://www.azpsych.org/

Arkansas

Barbara Stockton, Executive Director
Arkansas Psychiatric Society
P.O. Box 250910
Little Rock, AR 72225
(501) 663-6182

California

Barbara Gard, Executive Director
California Psychiatric Association
1400 K Street, Suite 302
Sacramento, CA 95814
(916) 442-5196
(916) 442-6515 fax
World Wide Web: http://www.calpsych.org/

Janice Clark Tagart, Executive Director
Northern California Psychiatric Society
1631 Ocean Avenue
San Francisco, CA 94112
(415) 334-2418
(415) 239-2533 fax

Holly Appelbaum, Executive Secretary
Orange County Psychiatric Society
300 South Flower Street
Orange, CA 92868
(714) 978-1160 or 3016
(714) 978-6039 fax

Amy Generaux, Executive Administrator
San Diego Psychiatric Society
3702 Ruffin Road, Suite 202
San Diego, CA 92123-3581
(619) 279-4586
(619) 279-4587 fax
World Wide Web: http://www.psychsd.org

Mindy Thelen, Administrative Director
Southern California Psychiatric Society
2999 Overland Avenue, Suite 116
Los Angeles, CA 90064
(310) 815-3650
(310) 815-3653 fax
E-mail: scps@sure.net

Colorado
Laura Michaels, Executive Director
Colorado Psychiatric Society
4596 East Iliff Avenue, Suite B
Denver, CO 80222
(303) 759-6045
(303) 759-6041 fax
E-mail: cps@nilenet.com

Connecticut
Jacquelyn Coleman, Executive Director
Connecticut Psychiatric Society
One Regency Drive, P.O. Box 30
Bloomfield, CT 06002
(860) 243-3977
(860) 286-0787 fax
World Wide Web: http://206.102.254.34/CTPS/index.html

Delaware
Mary LaJudice
Psychiatric Society of Delaware/Medical Society of Delaware
1925 Lovering Avenue
Wilmington, DE 19806-2166
(302) 658-7596
(302) 658-9669 fax

Florida
  Margo S. Adams, Executive Director
  Florida Psychiatric Society
  521 East Park Avenue
  Tallahassee, FL 32301-2524
  (904) 222-8404
  (904) 224-8406 fax
  E-mail: flapsy@aol.com
  World Wide Web: http://www.floridapsych.org

  Doris J. Shellow, Executive Director
  South Florida Psychiatric Society, Inc.
  P.O. Box 331266
  Miami, FL 33233-1266
  (305) 665-0130
  (305) 665-0390 fax

Georgia
  Tara Morrison, Executive Director
  Georgia Psychiatric Association
  938 Peachtree Street N.E.
  Atlanta, GA 30309
  (404) 876-7535, ext. 5091
  (404) 874-8651 fax

Hawaii
  Lydia Hardie, Executive Director
  Hawaii Psychiatric Medical Association
  1360 South Beretania Street
  Honolulu, HI 96814
  (808) 839-3070
  (808) 833-8165 fax
  E-mail: hpmalydia@aol.com

Idaho
  Michele Han, Executive Director
  Idaho District Branch of the American Psychiatric Association
  2683 Peregrine Place
  Boise, ID 83702
  (208) 342-4840

Illinois
  Sharon Gregg, Executive Director
  Dorothy Freeston, Membership Secretary
  Illinois Psychiatric Society
  20 North Michigan Avenue, Suite 700
  Chicago, IL 60602
  (312) 263-7391
  (312) 782-0553 fax

Indiana
  Janice A. Herring, Executive Secretary
  Indiana Psychiatric Society
  322 Canal Walk
  Indianapolis, IN 46202-3268
  (317) 261-2060, ext. 240
  (317) 261-2076 fax
  E-mail: jherring@ismanet.org

  Janet Peters
  Northern Indiana Psychiatric Society
  8585 Broadway, Suite 550
  Merrillville, IN 46410
  (219) 769-9122
  (219) 769-9127 fax

Iowa
  Barbara Walker, Executive Secretary
  Laura Allen, Executive Secretary
  Iowa Psychiatric Society
  1001 Grand Avenue
  West Des Moines, IA 50265
  (515) 223-2816
  (515) 223-8420 fax

Kansas
  Charles ("Chip") Wheelan, Executive Director
  Kansas Psychiatric Society
  623 Southwest Tenth Avenue
  Topeka, KS 66612-1615
  (913) 235-2383
  (913) 235-5114 fax

Kentucky
Ms. Theresa N. Walton, Executive Secretary
Kentucky Psychiatric Association
P.O. Box 198
Frankfort, KY 40602
(502) 695-4843
(502) 695-4441 fax

Louisiana
Charlene Smith, Executive Director
Louisiana Psychiatric Medical Association
P.O. Box 15765
New Orleans, LA 70175
(504) 891-1030 voice and fax

Maine
Esther M. Dudley, Executive Secretary
Maine Psychiatric Association
55 Grand Army Road
Whitefield, ME 04353
(207) 549-5786
E-mail: edudley@gwi.net

Maryland
Heidi E. Bunes, Executive Director
Maryland Psychiatric Society, Inc.
101 St. Paul Street, Suite 305
Baltimore, MD 21202
(410) 625-0232

Massachusetts
Dorothy Mooney, Executive Director
Massachusetts Psychiatric Society
40 Washington Street
Wellesley Hills, MA 02181
(617) 237-8100
(617) 237-7625 fax

Michigan
    Kathleen Williams, Executive Director
    Dodie Malloy, Membership Secretary
    Michigan Psychiatric Society
    15920 West Twelve Mile Road
    Southfield, MI 48076
    (810) 552-9300
    (810) 552-8790 fax

Minnesota
    Carol Eshelman, Executive Secretary
    Minnesota Psychiatric Society
    3433 Broadway Street, N.E., Suite 300
    Minneapolis, MN 55413-1761
    (612) 378-1875
    (612) 378-3875 fax

Mississippi
    Janis Borsig, Executive Secretary
    Mississippi Psychiatric Association
    2500 North State Street
    Jackson, MS 39216
    (601) 984-5808
    (601) 984-5842 fax
    E-mail: jan@fiona. umsmed.edu

Missouri
    Jan K. Frank, Executive Secretary
    Central Missouri Psychiatric Society
    111-B East Walnut
    Columbia, MO 65203-4164
    (573) 874-8985
    (573) 874-8986 fax

    Gordon Garrett, Ed.D., Executive Secretary
    Eastern Missouri Psychiatric Society
    3839 Lindell Boulevard
    St. Louis, MO 63108
    (314) 371-5225
    (314) 533-8601 fax

Ryan Laws, Associate Director
Western Missouri Psychiatric Society
3036 Gillham Road
Kansas City, MO 64108
(816) 531-8432
(816) 531-8438 fax

Montana
Virginia Hill, M.D., Executive Secretary
Montana Psychiatric Association
Drawer N
Warm Springs, MT 59756-0227
(406) 693-7000

Nebraska
Mindy McNeil, Executive Secretary
Nebraska Psychiatric Society
2500 California Plaza
Omaha, NE 68178
(402) 280-3179
(402) 280-1887 fax

Nevada
William Stone, M.D., Secretary/Treasurer
Nevada Association of Psychiatric Physicians
P.O. Box 12477
Las Vegas, NV 89112
(702) 877-6000
E-mail: nvapa@aol.com
World Wide Web:
http://members.aol.com/NVAPA/index.html

New Hampshire
Mary Pyne, Executive Secretary
New Hampshire Psychiatric Society
c/o New Hampshire Medical Society
7 North State Street
Concord, NH 03301
(603) 224-1900
(603) 226-2432 fax

New Jersey
   Carla A. Ross, Administrator
   New Jersey Psychiatric Association
   P.O. Box 8008
   Bridgewater, NJ 08807-8008
   (908) 685-0650
   (908) 725-8610 fax
   E-mail: njpa@mail.idt.net

New Mexico
   Marsha VerPloegh, Executive Secretary
   Psychiatric Medical Association of New Mexico
   801 Encino Place, N.E., Suite F-21
   Abuquerque, NM 87102
   (505) 224-7720
   (505) 224-7725 fax

New York
   Seth P. Stein, Esq., Executive Director and General Counsel
   New York State Psychiatric Association, Inc.
   100 Quentin Roosevelt Boulevard, Suite 509
   Garden City, NY 11530
   (516) 542-0077
   (516) 542-0094 fax
   E-mail: psychs4@aol.com
   World Wide Web: http://www.nyspsych.org

   Mary B. Cliffe, Executive Director
   Bronx District Branch of the American Psychiatric Association
   3801 Purchase Street
   Purchase, NY 10577
   (914) 946-3105
   (914) 946-3050 fax
   E-mail: pswapadb@aol.com

   Linda M. Majowka, Executive Director
   Brooklyn Psychiatric Society, Inc.
   Four Chimney Court
   Brookhaven, NY 11719
   (516) 286-9193 voice and fax

Noreen Lannon, Executive Secretary
Central New York District Branch
c/o Department of Psychiatry
750 East Adams Street
Syracuse, NY 13210
(315) 471-2716
(315) 464-3163 fax

Susan Shuryn, Executive Director
Genesee Valley Psychiatric Association
University of Rochester Medical Center
66 Hardison Road
Rochester, NY 14617-3852
(716) 234-1849
(716) 544-1257 fax

Jackie Cast, Executive Director
Greater Long Island Psychiatric Society
P.O. Box 3468
Farmingdale, NY 11735
(516) 249-1117
(516) 249-7202 fax
E-mail: jackie32@aol.com

Annette Patterson, Executive Secretary
Mid-Hudson Psychiatric Society
P.O. Box 3445
Poughkeepsie, NY 12603
(914) 452-5894 voice and fax

Rosalie Landy, Executive Director
New York County District Branch
150 East 58th Street, 31st Floor
New York, NY 10155-2396
(212) 421-4732/33/34
(212) 754-4671 fax
E-mail: nydbapa@mail.idt.net

Nancy Sykes, Executive Secretary
New York State Capital District Branch
American Psychiatric Association
P.O. Box 5
New Baltimore, NY 12124
(518) 756-8149

Carol Alsheimer, Executive Secretary
Northern New York District Branch
American Psychiatric Association
1400 Noyes at York
Utica, NY 13502
(315) 738-4405

Debbie Wessely, Executive Director
Queens County Psychiatric Society
47-04 159th Street
Flushing, NY 11358
(718) 461-8413

Mary B. Cliffe, Executive Director
Westchester County District Branch
American Psychiatric Association
3801 Purchase Street
Purchase, NY 10577
(914) 946-9008
(914) 946-3050 fax

Paul Ducker, M.D., Secretary
West Hudson District Branch
Dr. R.L. Yeager Center
Inpatient Unit, Bldg D
Pomona, NY 10970
(914) 364-2233
(914) 364-2214 fax
E-mail: drkroplick@MEM.po.com
World Wide Web: http://www.rfmh.org/whps

Donna Ball, Executive Secretary
Western New York Psychiatric Society
Erie County Medical Center, Department of Psychiatry
462 Grider Street
Buffalo, NY 14215
(716) 898-5941
(716) 898-4538 fax

North Carolina
   Katherine P. Hux, Executive Director
   North Carolina Psychiatric Association
   4917 Waters Edge, Suite 250
   Raleigh, NC 27606
   (919) 859-3370
   (919) 851-0044 fax
   E-mail: ncpalt@msn.com

North Dakota
   David Peske, Executive Director
   North Dakota District Branch
   P.O. Box 1198
   Bismarck, ND 58502-1198
   (701) 223-9475
   (701) 223-9476 fax

Ohio
   Philip Workman, Executive Director
   Ohio Psychiatric Association
   1480 West Lane Avenue, Suite F
   Columbus, OH 43221
   (614) 481-7555
   (614) 481-7559 fax
   E-mail: paworkman@aol.com
   World Wide Web: http://users.aol.com/ohiopsych/opa.htm

Oklahoma
   Claudene Channell, Executive Secretary
   Oklahoma Psychiatric Association
   P.O. Box 1328
   Norman, OK 73070
   (405) 360-5066

Oregon
   John H. McCulley, Executive Secretary
   Oregon Psychiatric Association
   P.O. Box 2042
   Salem, OR 97308
   (503) 370-7019 or 800-533-7031 (within Oregon only)
   (503) 399-8082 fax

Pennsylvania
Gwen Lehman, Executive Director
Pennsylvania Psychiatric Society
777 East Park Drive
P.O. Box 8820
Harrisburg, PA 17105
(717) 558-7750 or 800-422-2900 (within Pennsylvania only)
(717) 558-7841 fax

Rhode Island
Edwina Rego, Membership Secretary
Rhode Island Psychiatric Society
106 Francis Street
Providence, RI 02903
(401) 331-1450
(401) 751-8050 fax
World Wide Web: http://www.butler.org/~psy/RIPS/

South Carolina
Debbie Shealy, Executive Director
Tara Smith, Membership Coordinator
South Carolina Psychiatric Association
P.O. Box 11188
Columbia, SC 29211
(803) 798-6207

South Dakota
Kate Naylor, Executive Secretary
South Dakota Psychiatric Association
1400 West 22nd Street
Sioux Falls, SD 57105
(605) 357-1585
(605) 357-1311 fax
E-mail: knaylor@sunflowr.usd.edu

Tennessee
Chris Fitzpatrick, Executive Director
Tennessee Psychiatric Association
209 Tenth Avenue South, Suite 506
Nashville, TN 37203
(615) 255-3102
(615) 254-1186 fax

Texas
   John Bush, Executive Director
   Debbie Sundberg, Assistant Director
   Texas Society of Psychiatric Physicians
   401 West 15th, Suite 675
   Austin, TX 78701
   (512) 478-0605
   (512) 478-5223 fax

Utah
   Paige De Mille, Executive Director
   Utah Psychiatric Association
   540 East 500 South
   Salt Lake City, UT 84102
   (801) 355-7477
   (801) 532-1550 fax

Vermont
   Ada Bagalio, Administrative Secretary
   Vermont Psychiatric Association
   c/o Vermont State Medical Society
   P.O. Box 1457
   Montpelier, VT 05601
   (802) 223-7898
   (802) 223-1201 fax

Virginia
   Ruth McDonough, Executive Secretary
   Psychiatric Society of Virginia, Inc.
   209 Culpeper Road
   Richmond, VA 23229
   (804) 282-1231
   (804) 282-5621 fax

Washington, DC
   Alvin Golub, Executive Director
   Rosemary Polley, Executive Secretary
   Washington Psychiatric Society
   1400 K Street, N.W.
   Washington, DC 20005
   (202) 682-6159 or 6192
   (202) 682-6369 fax

Washington State
   Ronna Schwalk, Staff Assistant
   Washington State Psychiatric Association
   901 Boren, Suite 1731
   Seattle, WA 98104
   (206) 223-7709 or 2281
   (206) 223-1375 fax

West Virginia
   Lynn Wilson, Executive Secretary
   West Virginia Psychiatric Association
   Chestnut Ridge Hospital
   930 Chestnut Ridge Road
   Morgantown, WV 26505
   (304) 293-3970
   (304) 293-5555 fax

Wisconsin
   Edward Levin, Executive Secretary
   Wisconsin Psychiatric Association
   P.O. Box 1109
   Madison, WI 53701
   (608) 257-6781
   (608) 283-5401 fax

Wyoming
   Jean Davis, Executive Secretary
   Wyoming Psychiatric Society
   2521 East 15th Street
   Casper, WY 82609
   (307) 237-7444

United States Armed Services
   Barbara Ross, Executive Secretary
   Society of Uniformed Services Psychiatrists
   15000 East Way Drive
   Silver Spring, MD 20905
   (301) 654-6639

Puerto Rico

Mildred Figueroa, Chief Executive Officer
Puerto Rico Psychiatric Society
Ashford Medical Center, Suite 209-B
Condado, PR 00907
(909) 739-5555
(809) 739-5544 fax
World Wide Web: http://members, tripod.com/~nesile/
PRPShome.html

Canada

Ontario
Heather Young, Executive Secretary
Ontario District Branch
3 Langbourne Place
Don Mills, ON M3B 1A8
(416) 445-9616
(416) 465-9585 fax
E-mail: odbapa@rogers.wave.ca

Quebec and Eastern Canada
Lise Godbout
c/o Jacques Bouchard, M.D., Secretary
Quebec and Eastern Canada District Branch
3120 Boulevard Taschereau
Greenfield Park, PQ J4V 2H1
(514) 466-5060
(514) 466-1540 fax
E-mail: godboe@cycor.ca

Western Canada
Jennie Mould, Membership Secretary
Western Canada District Branch
115-1665 West Broadway
Vancouver, BC V6J 5A4
(604) 736-5551
(604) 736-3987 fax

Index